TOWARD THE 21st CENTURY:
EDUCATION FOR A CHANGING WORLD

TOWARD THE 21st CENTURY:
EDUCATION FOR A CHANGING WORLD

EDWIN O. REISCHAUER

Vintage Books
A Division of Random House, New York

FIRST VINTAGE BOOKS EDITION, October 1974

Library of Congress Cataloging in Publication Data
Reischauer, Edwin Oldfather, 1910–
    Toward the 21st century; education for a changing world.
    "A portion of this book was adapted from the 1973 Year book, covering the events of 1972."
    1. International relations.   I. Title.
[JX1395.R4 1974]   327   74–3251
ISBN 0–394–71159–9

Contents

PART ONE
THE PROBLEM

The large theme of this small book is that we need a profound reshaping of education if mankind is to survive in the sort of world that is fast evolving. In all human affairs, the speed of change seems constantly to accelerate and the complexity of relationships to multiply. This is particularly true in international relations, because the forward rush of technology is fast eliminating the cushioning space that once existed between the diverse nations and contrasting cultures of the world. Take for example instantaneous global communications that penetrate our homes, networks of jet airplane routes that bring the very ends of the world within a few hours of each other, giant ships that have drastically reduced the costs of oceanic transportation and thus have brought about a massive upsurge in worldwide economic contacts, and intercontinental nuclear missiles of unimaginable destructiveness, to mention only a few items.

The result of all this is a rapid increase in interdependence but also of tensions. While the world is in the process of becoming a single great mass of humanity—a global community, as it is sometimes called—the very diverse national and cultural groupings that make up the world's population retain attitudes and habits more appropriate to a different technological age, when the contrasting civilizations existed far removed from one another and the well-being of most individuals was determined within largely self-contained nations, or even smaller communities. The continuance of such parochial attitudes in an interdependent, closely knit world would probably spell catastrophe. Basically this is an educational problem.

Before long, humanity will face many grave difficulties that can only be solved on a global scale. For this there must be a much higher degree of understanding and a far greater capacity for cooperation between disparate peoples and nations than exist now. Education, however, as it is presently conducted in this country—and in every other country in the world, for that matter—is not moving rapidly enough in the right direction to produce the knowledge about the outside world and the attitudes toward other peoples that may be essential for human survival within a generation or two. This, I feel, is a much greater international problem than the military balance of power that absorbs so much of our attention today.

Stated in these rough and sweeping terms, my thesis revolves around a single great problem, but on closer analysis it breaks down into two quite separate sets of questions. The one concerns current world trends and the nature of the problems these will pose for mankind in the decades ahead. These questions I discuss in Part Two. The other centers on the educational responses these world trends and looming problems call for. These I take up in Part Three. This leaves Part One for a brief introductory statement of the theme as a whole, some discussion of the nature and limitations of this study, and a consideration of the urgency of the problem we face.

No one can peer into the murky future and discern clearly where the world is headed or what its educational needs may be. All that one can do is to make some educated guesses based on past and current trends. This book constitutes no more than a set of such judgments, illustrated by a few specific examples but in no sense proved by them.

One could, of course, analyze in much greater detail than I have the multitudinous aspects of international relations as they have developed in the past and as they appear today. These problems could be dissected region by region, country by country, and phase by phase—the military, political, economic, technological, sociological, cultural, and ideological, and all the many facets of each of these general categories. It would not be hard to amass endless tables of statistics. These in turn could be made to seem more authoritative by running them through computers to produce correlation coefficients, charts, and statistically expressed hypotheses. The result, of course, would be not an essay but a veritable library of weighty tomes. And even then the projections about the future and its problems would still just be hypotheses, limited by the perceptions of the person who had assembled the facts and programmed the computer—that is, by the types of problems he was able to perceive, the data he decided to select, the variables he chose to use in his models, and the somewhat arbitrary weightings he gave to them. There would be a great deal of factual material, perhaps enough to obscure rather than clarify the points that are most important. But the final conclusions would still be essentially unprovable suppositions deriving from fallible human judgment.

The problem is not a lack of data. We are already floundering in a sea of facts and statistics. The real problem is how the facts fit together in the dynamic process that is shaping man's future. In approaching the subject, therefore, I have chosen to avoid a detailed, across-the-board presentation of international relations and have limited facts and statistics to a minimum. They rapidly become out of date in any case. Instead, I have attempted to take a wide look at the direction of historical flow in human affairs and to explain through a few illustrations what would seem to be the basic problems in international relations now and in the foreseeable future. On the basis of these judgments, then, I have tried to outline the educational responses that would seem necessary.

I have approached the problem posed in this book as a historian, accustomed to study developments over extensive periods of time, and therefore I have emphasized long-range general trends rather than immediate specific problems. In fact, I have consciously attempted to avoid being diverted from these trends by the specific issues of the moment. It is all too common for both scholars and political leaders to admit in theory the existence of these long-range problems but to disregard them in practice for other more immediate concerns, such as current international negotiations on more specific points, the latest weapons needed for defense, and new trade agreements or tariff policies designed to affect next year's balance of payments. While these all are important in themselves, I am concerned with them here merely as illustrations of the long-range problems and as way stations either to a resolution of these problems or to a breakdown in the effort to cope with them. Since my special interests have always lain in Japan and East Asia, my insights and illustrations, both on immediate issues and on long-range trends, have been drawn in large part from that region, which I believe shows the present tensions and looming problems of the world as clearly as any.

I realize that my analysis of world trends and emerging global problems can easily be faulted by others with different angles of vision and areas of primary concern. Since I am no specialist on elementary and secondary education, I am even more open to criticism in that field. My picture of the evolving world and suggestions for education may be overdrawn; they undoubtedly are sketchy and limited. We are all blind men when we face the great elephant of the contemporary world, unable to comprehend fully the relationship between its various parts, much less the complexities of its crinkled folds.

Some of these weaknesses could have been avoided or at least lessened if this book had been the product of a team. A committee of experts with complementary specialties could have produced a far more balanced and judicious statement. But I chose not to approach the problem in this way. The well-rounded product of team effort, in losing its rough edges, can all too easily lose its sharpness of statement. The homogenized blend of group wisdom, in gaining smoothness, often loses flavor. My purpose is not to present a definitive analysis of the world's future and a blueprint for education but to call attention to the problems. For this a single sharp bugle call, however imperfect, may be more effective than a smoother and more complexly orchestrated symphony.

Actually, most of my judgments about the prospects for the world and the needs in education are not very new or revolutionary. They are widely shared by others who have thought about such matters, though they might prefer to formulate these problems somewhat differently. The bulk of Americans and people in other countries, however, have not really given serious attention to such questions. Even among those who have, there is a tendency either to be too complacent about the progress we are making toward solving them or else to believe that domestic concerns are so much more pressing that we must concentrate our attention largely on them and, at least for a while, let global problems and the resulting educational needs take care of themselves. But neither complacency nor benign neglect will do.

I would not for a moment deny the importance and urgency of solving the multitudinous and sometimes bewildering domestic problems we face. In fact, a strong case could be made that, unless we do much better than we have in handling these, our own country will prove unviable, regardless of what happens in our relations with the rest of the world. We can all see that, in a society becoming ever more complex and intricately interrelated, we must acquire new attitudes in relations between the races, between ethnic and religious communities, geographic regions, are groupings, and even between the sexes. Clearly, our old image of ourselves as rugged individualists and daring frontiersmen, while possibly useful in the past, when Americans of an earlier age explored and developed a vast new land, is ill adapted to the realities of life for most Americans in the late twentieth century. We obviously must rethink our proud local autonomies that have permitted the segregation of wealth from poverty and thus have contributed to the disaster of the cities. We must find a better balance between economic growth and the preservation of our environment, between a fair distribution of wealth and opportunity and the maintenance of basic individual freedoms, and between the identity of the individual and the complexity and anonymity of modern mass society. We all run the danger of becoming swallowed up by an increasingly mechanized and depersonalized system, bound down by proliferating red tape, and smothered in a rising sludge of bureaucratic obfuscation. In short, we need a reassessment of our basic values, new concepts of social responsibility, and a new sense of self-identity, perhaps based on a new type of self-discipline. It is all too possible that the fast-increasing complexities, pressures, and frustrations of contemporary life will bring on a neurotic breakdown of our whole society.

In emphasizing the importance of global problems and arguing the urgency of the reform of education about international matters, I do not mean to suggest that these other problems are less important. From my own particular perspective as a student of East Asia, I can see, perhaps more clearly than others do, our need to develop some of the social skills and attitudes the Chinese and Japanese have achieved. I have in mind the traditional Chinese balance within each individual between his activist role in society and his personal, esthetic life—what some have called the yin-yang duality of personality—and the skill of the Japanese in minimizing personal clashes through consensual group decisions, combined with their ability to armor themselves against the loneliness and anomie of modern urban life by a relevant self-identity achieved through group affiliations.

The relative importance of domestic and international problems is not the question. We must continue to address ourselves simultaneously to both. Life does not usually permit a choice between problems. The driver of a car can never forget about the steering wheel in order to concentrate his attention more fully on the accelerator. We will either survive by handling both our domestic and foreign problems with adequate skill, or else we will fail totally. In terms of the ultimate outcome, it would make no difference which of the two areas first showed signs of collapse.

I am writing only about global problems and the international dimension in education primarily because this is closer to my own area of special interest and knowledge, but also for a second reason. The needs in this field, I believe, are much less clearly perceived than in domestic problems. On the latter we are all in a sense experts, because we live in the midst of them. Our educational system is pressed upon by domestic problems from all sides. And formal education is not the only shaper of new attitudes and approaches. It may not even be the major one. Even if the school system failed to adapt to the needs, the rest of society might still respond to the problems and help reshape our thinking and conduct.

In the case of foreign affairs, none of this is true. Few people have specialized knowledge. The problems seem remote. In a large country like the United States, people in peacetime feel the foreign impact only vaguely and indirectly. They only seem to notice when they sense a direct military or economic threat to them or when their loved ones are sent to die overseas. And then they react emotionally and probably unwisely, out of fear and a lack of understanding. It therefore requires a much more special effort in foreign affairs than in domestic matters to make people aware of the problems and help them adjust to them wisely. In other words, a conscious educational undertaking is necessary.

It is harder to argue against complacency over the progress we already are making in preparing ourselves for a more international and eventually global world community. American education has come a long way in this regard during the generation since World War II and is continuing to move rapidly in the right direction. No one could reasonably argue that letting things continue as they are in this field would lead to any great international crisis or catastrophe within the next decade or two. Benign neglect therefore might seem a reasonable attitude —given all the other problems besetting our educational system.

There are, however, two basic flaws in this argument. Our educational progress in preparing ourselves for a more international and eventually global world community is considerably less than appears on the surface.

The advance during the past quarter century may have been spectacular in percentage terms, but this is only because the starting point was close to zero. Most of the progress, moreover, has been made where it is most visible —in the types of schools patronized by the affluent middle class of the metropolitan suburbs. But the great bulk of American schoolchildren are still not much affected. They absorb little real knowledge of peoples and nations with different cultural backgrounds and gain little perception of the growing interdependence of mankind and the necessity of developing a sense of world community. In a democracy, of course, the determining factor in political decisions is likely to be the basic emotional reactions of the masses rather than the more sophisticated perceptions of the educational élite.

The other flaw in the argument is the time factor. The crucial period is not the next decade or two. It seems probable that the world can drift that long without catastrophe. The time of serious concern, when present trends are likely to produce crisis conditions, lies a generation or two ahead—say thirty to sixty years from now. But the important point is that the drift of the next two decades could prove decisive in determining how well we meet these crises when they come. During these years may come the point of no return, when we let ourselves be caught in currents that lead to a still distant but increasingly unavoidable waterfall of human events, instead of trying to guide our destiny into safer waters while this is still possible.

The inevitable time lag in the educational process makes these next few decades all the more crucial for the generations that lie ahead. The child entering first grade this year will not be a member of the voting public for well over a decade. He is not likely to have gotten well started on his career for two decades or more. His most important period as a leader or a molder of opinion, if he ever achieves such levels of prominence, lies roughly three to six decades ahead. During the intervening years he will no doubt still be learning, but his basic attitudes are likely to have been strongly conditioned, if not completely shaped, by the perceptions and prejudices he is absorbing now.

Education thus has at least a generation of time lag automatically built into it. If it in turn is somewhat behind the times, as is so frequently the situation, the lag can be still greater. We have seen all too many historical examples when national leaders and the general public behind them responded to new international problems with outmoded perceptions and methods. Our recent disaster in Vietnam is a particularly clear case in point. With the accelerating speed of change in the world, this generation gap in education becomes more serious all the time. It is frightening to imagine American leaders and the voting public facing global problems as these will probably develop during the first half of the twenty-first century with the basic attitudes and emotions about the rest of the world that American education and environmental influences are likely to instill in most of them today. In the field of education, there is no time for relaxed inattention, because the twenty-first century and its problems are already here.

It is, of course, a tall order to ask education to prepare for the conditions and problems of the twenty-first century. In the past, efforts at foretelling where humanity was heading and preparing men for this journey were left to prophets, religious leaders, and philosophers. Their success in transmitting their insights to others was usually quite limited, and in any case their insights were often far from accurate. How can mass education hope to perform the task any better? How can we, on the basis of present knowledge and attitudes, estimate what knowledge and attitudes may be necessary even ten years hence? It may seem to be folly to inject such an idea into education. But it is much more certain folly not to do so. In that case, at least one thing seems predictable and that is disaster for mankind.

Human requirements in the past have from time to time forced major revisions in the concepts and practices of education. Perhaps we need such a restructuring of education today. In primitive times, education was little more than the observation and imitation by the young of the skills and attitudes of their elders, and this still remains a basic part of education today. In time, the accumulation of knowledge and specialization of functions required more focused efforts to transmit skills, attitudes, and special lore, especially in such fields as religion. The development of writing probably marked a great watershed in education, because it permitted a wide expansion of accumulated knowledge, and reading and writing were not skills to be acquired merely by observing others practice them. In time a more formal type of education—that is, schools with professional teachers—became necessary. This eventually grew into huge national school systems and a great variety of specialized institutions transmitting the very advanced skills without which a complex society would collapse into chaos.

Throughout the long history of education, the emphasis inevitably has been on the transmission of knowledge, skills, and attitudes already developed. All too often the primary focus was more on a religion inherited from the past, or on the lore of some supposed "golden age" of antiquity and its languages, than on contemporary problems. This was as true in the great civilizations of India and China as in the Islamic world and the West. Only in comparatively recent times has education become much concerned with contemporary problems and associated with ongoing progress in knowledge and skills. And the association with progress took place for the most part only at the highest levels of education. Elementary, secondary, and even most of so-called higher education tended to lag decades behind, usually content with the levels of knowledge attained in the preceding generation and passing on already outmoded attitudes.

One cannot say that this static, sometimes backward-looking approach to education did not work in the past. The human race has muddled through with reasonable success up until now with this sort of education. But clearly this is no longer adequate. Change is now so rapid and drastic that future generations, if given an education based on the already somewhat outdated perceptions of the preceding generation, may not be able to adjust in time to the new conditions. And the rate of change goes on accelerating at an alarming pace. If the human life span were shorter—say ten years to reach maturity and ten years of productive life—the succession of generations might be fast enough to keep up with the rate of change, at least for a little while longer. But in this, as in so much else, we are stuck with our biological limitations. We are the only people we've got.

Obviously we must reduce, or if possible eliminate, the lag between the bulk of formal education and the forward edge of knowledge and attitudes. This is a problem basically of organization—of the more rapid transmittal of knowledge and attitudes from the thinkers and discoverers to the educational process and a better system of keeping teachers up to date through a constant process of retraining. We also must make an effort to focus education, not just on the transmission of past knowledge and skills, but on the problems that appear to be unfolding ahead of us. We seem to be entering a new stage in history in which we must make a conscious attempt to structure formal education so that it better prepares the younger generation for a fast-changing future.

I have no neat formulae for how this is to be done, though I do explore in Part Three some of the problems involved. But first we must attempt to see where the world is heading, what problems this direction of motion will pose for mankind, and how these may best be met; without some idea of such matters, we will have no way of knowing what may be needed of education.

PART TWO

THE EMERGING
WORLD COMMUNITY

1 ☝ TOWARD A UNITARY WORLD

One of the basic assumptions of this book is that the world is rapidly shrinking into a single vast unit which will survive as a whole—that is, as a global community—or not at all. This is a sweeping judgment that is beyond definitive proof, but the trends of history point clearly in this direction.

Some people appear to think that "one world" and the unified international community this term implies are already realities, but this is still far from true. It is equally wrong, however, to assume that the concept is all humbug, as the more cynical or the more parochial would have it. The world gives every sign of drawing rapidly together as a complexly interrelated and interdependent unit. The only question is whether it will be a peaceful and therefore viable "one world" when this comes about, or whether, on formation, it will explode like a nuclear pile that has reached a critical mass, destroying civilization in the process and conceivably exterminating all human life. Since the unification of the world is proceeding at an ever more rapid rate, we may not have long to wait for the answer, though just what "we" will mean in the one case is hard to judge.

If we glance back at history, we can discern the rapidly accelerating pace at which the world is drawing together. Primitive hunting and gathering man lived not in "one world" but in a myriad of isolated, family-like groups, which were only slightly in touch with even close neighbors and virtually unaffected by groups living at any great distance. Agriculture produced larger, more complex communities and eventually city states and small empires, which rubbed together in military conflict with their immediate neighbors and traded even further afield. There was, for example, a considerable exchange of goods between Sumer in Mesopotamia and the cities of the Indus Valley in the northwestern corner of the Indian subcontinent, even though these areas are separated by some 1,400 miles of sea routes and even more forbidding mountains and deserts. But contact between truly distant regions, such as Egypt and China, was either nonexistent or such a slow and indirect process that neither side was aware of it.

Gradually interaction increased. In the centuries just before and after the time of Christ, the great classic empires of the Mediterranean area, the Indian subcontinent, and China not only brought together diverse areas and large populations under a single rule but also developed more trade and other contacts than had existed before between these far-separated islands of high civilization. Alexander the Great actually penetrated to India in 327 B.C. in his search for more worlds to conquer. As a result of the Roman demand for Chinese silk, the so-called silk road of caravan trade developed between the Mediterranean and China through Central Asia, and across it goods and influences passed in both directions.

From their conquests in Central Asia, the Chinese were vaguely aware of Rome—they called it Great Ch'in—and some traders, apparently from the Roman Orient, are recorded in A.D. 166 as having come by sea to the southern borders of the Chinese Empire in what is now Vietnam. But the classic civilizations were still essentially separate worlds. The great contemporaneous empires of Rome in the Mediterranean area, of the Maurya, Asoka, and the Kushan in the Indian area, and the two Han Dynasties in China never came into direct contact with one another.

As the "silk road" showed, the seminomadic peoples that lived between the three great nodes of high agricultural civilization served as a trade link between them. When the great classic empires waned and these seminomads gained in military strength through cavalry tactics, they also gave the great sedentary civilizations a common strategic problem. Drawn by the wealth of the agricultural regions, the nomads repeatedly pillaged these areas or settled down to rule over them. On the whole, the greater population and tighter political organization of China made it a harder region to penetrate than were the Middle East and India. In any case, the chief motion of nomad conquest was from east to west, as wave after wave of seminomads from East Asia—Huns, Turks, and Mongols—rolled with disastrous force westward into the histories of India, the Middle East, and Eastern Europe. A return wave of religion rolled eastward through Central Asia over the same routes of trade and conquest. Buddhism in the first seven centuries of the Christian era spread from India throughout East Asia. Islam, originating in the seventh century in Arabia on the southeastern edge of the Mediterranean world, penetrated by land deep into India and through Central Asia to the northwestern corner of China.

For well over a millennium the seminomadic peoples of Central Asia served as the chief contact between the great centers of high civilization, as traders, as transmitters of religions and other cultural influences, and as conquerors. The Mongols of the thirteenth and fourteenth centuries, subduing China and Korea to the east and conquering deep into the Middle East and Russia to the west, ruled over a larger proportion of the world's population and its known land area than any empire before or since. The Mongol Empire also marked the high point in this phase of transcontinental contacts between the great classic areas of civilization. It was in the late thirteenth century that the Venetian Marco Polo was able to travel through the vast domains of the Mongol Khan, enter his service in Peking, and thus get his dazzling view of the glories of China, then at the height of its period of world leadership in economic wealth, technical skills, and social and political organization.

In the long run, however, ships proved much more important than caravans in bringing the world together. Coastal trading within the Mediterranean area and between it and India goes back to antiquity, and by the Christian era merchant ships had begun to venture around the long southward dangling peninsula of Southeast Asia to the southern coast of China. But large-scale oceanic trade did not commence until around the seventh and eighth centuries. At first it was largely between the various regions of Asia, particularly between the Middle East, India, and China. It was pushed on the one side by the expansionist energies of Moslem Persians and Arabs and pulled on the other side by the lure of China's great wealth and the excellence of its manufactures, especially porcelains and silks. By the eleventh and twelfth centuries, it had grown to great proportions. In the early phases of the coastal Asian trade, Hinduism and Buddhism were carried by it to Southeast Asia. In the fifteenth century, it brought Islam also to this region.

At the end of the fifteenth century, the Europeans, after probing their way around Africa, broke in on this already flourishing trade along the coasts of Asia and, with their now sturdier vessels and greater firepower, quickly became masters over much of it. At almost the same time they also discovered the Americas and circumnavigated the globe. Thus by the early sixteenth century a new age was clearly dawning. The major areas of high civilization had come into direct contact with one another by sea, and man's hitherto flat habitat had curled up to form a giant ball. In these two ways the world had started to draw together into a single great community.

The next three centuries saw an increasing domination of international trade by the Europeans and their over-running of the Americas and in time the Australian continent. European nations established footholds around the globe and extended their petty rivalries at home into military contests for leadership in the Western Hemisphere and even in India and Southeast Asia. The age of European imperialism had dawned.

The bulk of the people of the world, however, still

lived in isolated cultural and national compartments, little affected by what went on elsewhere in the world. Far-flung conquests and trade had some impact on the economies and thought of Europe, but only as external, peripheral stimuli. The influence of these relations on the lives and thought of most of the other people was much less. Despite the growing British involvement in India, for example, Englishmen and Indians continued to live in two almost completely separate worlds. The same could be said of Dutchmen and Indonesians. The Middle East remained impotent to influence Europe and determinedly resistant to Western penetration. Except for its southern tip, Africa was almost untouched. Continental Southeast Asia still remained relatively free of Western domination. China, with close to one-quarter of all mankind, succeeded in keeping the rest of the world at arm's length, confining Western trade and residence to two tiny contact points in the deep south, at Macao and Canton. Korea was still almost entirely secluded except for its relations with China. And the Japanese, after exuberantly exchanging goods with the Europeans in the latter half of the sixteenth century, enthusiastically adopting their military technology, and flirting with Christianity, relapsed by 1639 into a harsh and entirely effective self-isolation. At the start of the nineteenth century, "one world" was not much closer to being a reality than it had been at the beginning of the sixteenth.

The nineteenth century and particularly its second half, however, saw a rapid advance to a new stage in international relations and with it another clear shrinking of the globe. There were a variety of factors behind this change. One was the mechanization of production in the West, which suddenly gave it a great economic advantage over the rest of the world in certain types of industrial products. Another was the concomitant strengthening of the national unit in the West as a military as well as economic force. More specifically, the application of steam power to navigation greatly increased Western domination of the seas and the capacity to transport both military power and the fruits of machine production to distant shores.

Western political domination and economic exploitation of areas already colonial, such as India and Indonesia, increased greatly, and patterns of economic domination were established in politically free but economically weak areas like Latin America. France and Britain established control over large areas in the Middle East and divided up much of continental Southeast Asia between them. Africa was carved up and, with the exception of Ethiopia and Liberia, parceled out to voracious European imperial powers. In a series of wars and incidents, beginning in 1839, China was pried open bit by bit to Western economic, cultural, and political penetration, with ultimately disastrous consequences for the traditional economy, political system, and social order. Japan similarly was forced by Commodore Perry of the American Navy to open its doors in 1854, and Korea had to follow suit within a few decades. European rivalries and the European balance of power were spread to the whole world. A new naval port or merely a coaling station in East Asia, a more rigid treaty with a Middle Eastern ruler, a new economic concession in Latin America, or a new chunk of jungle terrain in Africa were all factored into European power rivalries, which were seen as precariously balanced around the globe.

By the early twentieth century it was clear that the world had become far more unitary than it had ever been before. It also seemed to most observers that this had been accomplished by the swallowing of the rest of the world by the West. Except for the countries of East Asia —China, Japan, and Korea—most of the world was under Western rule, and even the East Asian states had been forced to accommodate to a world environment determined by Western industrial power, Western culture, and Western concepts of international organization. To Occidental eyes, a world made one through Western domination seemed both inevitable and entirely right. History, however, was to prove this concept a delusion. The world was much too big an ox to be swallowed by the Western frog, much less digested. Most people in the world were not really part of the "one world" of Western culture and a Europe-centered balance of power.

The extension of Western power throughout the world in the second half of the nineteenth century had been paralleled by another significant development. This was the Japanese response to the Western challenge. Japan, forced by the United States in 1854 to open its closed doors, had shown itself capable of utilizing the new technology, institutions, and national solidarity of the West to build sufficient industrial and military power to preserve its independence and start to compete with the West on the latter's own terms. In 1868, Japan embarked on an amazing political and social transformation of its feudal society; slowly over the decades it became competitive with the West in one field of industry after another; by 1894–5 it had developed sufficient modern military power to defeat China and start its own empire through the seizure of Taiwan and the subsequent annexation of Korea in 1910; in 1904–5 it came into conflict with Russia, one of the greatest European powers, and emerged victorious. All this showed that the eventual "one world" might prove to be something more than just an expanded West.

Japan's victory over Russia sent intellectual shock waves throughout Asia. There had been desultory resistance to Western political domination all along and a dogged determination to cling to old ways, but now it seemed possible that any Asian country, if it could only pull itself together as a national unit and "modernize" its economy and institutions, as Japan had done, could regain its freedom and achieve a self-respecting place in the world community. Self-conscious nationalist movements appeared in many countries. Even though they were pitifully small and weak at first, they were to grow, until in the years following World War II they were able to sweep Western imperial domination out of all of Asia and most of Africa. The Japanese reaction to the Western challenge and the response of other non-Western nations to Japan's success were to prove a more lasting part of the emerging "one world" than were the Western empires.

The period of the two so-called world wars and the two decades between them may be seen as another significant new stage in the evolution of a world community. The very name "World War" for the great European conflict of 1914–18 shows the growing consciousness of a unitary world at the time, even though it really is a misnomer. The war did extend into a corner of the Middle East, because of Turkey's alliance with Germany, but this was a side show; otherwise, the spread of the war beyond Europe was only a by-product of the extension of European power around the globe in earlier years. The United States, Canada, Australia, and New Zealand, all extensions of English-speaking peoples overseas, became deeply involved by sending troops to the battle zones in Europe and the Middle East; Asian and African colonial troops were brought to Europe; and the German colonies in Africa and the Pacific were seized by their enemies, specifically by the Japanese in the case of the German foothold in China and the islands of the North Pacific. But for most of the peoples of the world, this was not their war, and many probably remained quite oblivious to it.

Still, World War I came closer to being a truly global conflict than any previous war in history, and from it came worldwide shocks which showed that the world was indeed becoming more unitary. The sending of railway rolling stock from India to the Middle East produced a famine in the subcontinent because of the weakening of the distribution system. The disappearance of European goods from Asian markets gave a tremendous stimulus to the growth of Japan's export industries. The Russian Revolution of 1917, resulting from the collapse of the czarist régime during the war, produced waves of new ideas and aspirations that beat with varying force on most nations, Western or non-Western, throughout the whole world. Perhaps the clearest sign of the new age was the effort at its end to establish a world order through the creation of the League of Nations. Even though the concept was not an entirely new one, the understanding and abilities of the statesmen of the time proved far from adequate for the task. Still, the scale and seriousness of the attempt showed that there was a much broader realization of the needs for an organized world order than ever before.

The growing oneness of the world was demonstrated perhaps more clearly in the worldwide economic doldrums of the 1920's and the great depression that fell like a pall over the world at the end of the decade. The economic well-being of people in almost all parts of the world was becoming increasingly influenced by economic conditions elsewhere, even if most people remained only dimly aware of this growing interdependence. Economic interactions between nations and regions had existed for some centuries, but never before on a global scale or in such intensity. A simple Malayan tapper of rubber trees might find his food supply dependent on the quantity of tires Americans and Europeans would buy. American and European industrialists and workers felt threatened by cheap Japanese manufactured goods, while Japanese businessmen began to say that, if New York sneezed, Japan would catch pneumonia. The inability of the economists and statesmen of the period to find international solutions to the worldwide trade problem prolonged the agony well into the 1930's, until it gradually became a part of even more serious world tensions.

Out of the fears and frictions of the great depression emerged a determined effort by the more rapidly growing powers to achieve security for themselves and a "place in the sun" by the creation of great regional hegemonies. As they saw the situation, accidents of history and geography had unfairly given domination over the bulk of the world to certain powers—the great sea empires of the British and French and the land empires of the Russians and Americans. They saw themselves by comparison as "have-nots" who deserved better. The Germans aspired to domination over Western Europe, with perhaps a vassal empire left to the Italians in the Mediterranean and North Africa, while the Japanese aimed at the most populous empire the world had ever seen—close to a billion people in what they euphemistically called the "Greater East Asia Co-Prosperity Sphere." The Germans and Japanese were willing, at least for the time being, to leave the broad lands of the Soviet Union to the Russians and the Americas to the United States; but neither the Americans nor the Russians could see such a regionally divided world as promising security for themselves or peace for the world, and of course the British, French, Chinese, and other proposed helots of German and Japanese rule were ready to put up a desperate resistance. War resulted, starting in East Asia in 1937, in Europe in 1939, and involving the United States in 1941.

World War II was truly a "world war." It was fought throughout most of Europe and deep into the heart of Russia, across the whole of North Africa, from the eastern borders of India throughout Southeast Asia and all of East Asia, and far across the vast expanses of the Pacific. Virtually all the peoples of the world were deeply affected by it in one way or another, and the closing phases showed that an entirely new era in international relations was dawning. The beginning of the nuclear age signaled another abrupt contraction of the size of the globe.

World War I had been fought, at least by some, as the "war to end war." World War II, through the nuclear weapons it helped develop, actually became the war that foretold the end either of war between major powers or of civilization. Suspicion and rivalry between nuclear powers became, not the old game of balance of power, but a worldwide balance of terror determining the survival of humanity. "One world" of life or death—a common global destiny for mankind—had suddenly become a reality.

The fear of nuclear destruction has not been the only factor to render the world much more unified since World War II. International contacts of all sorts have expanded vastly. Trade and every other form of economic interdependence have grown by quantum jumps in most of the world. The economic interrelationships that made the great depression of the interwar years a worldwide phenomenon have multiplied many times over since then. The once thin and halting flow of communications between nations and regions has become an incessant flood. The international movement of officials, businessmen, students, laborers seeking employment, and casual tourists has grown to proportions undreamed of before.

At the close of World War II, many people showed at least a dim awareness that the world had entered a new age. The most obvious sign of this was the new and much more determined effort to achieve a world order—this time through the United Nations. Though far from being an effective mechanism, except for peripheral and not highly controversial issues, the United Nations more than a quarter century after its birth still stays alive as a hope. By contrast the League of Nations had heard its death knell in the Manchurian Incident of 1931, only a little over a decade after its inception, and before it completed its second decade another world war had broken out.

Living as we do in the midst of a postwar age, it is difficult to see this era clearly in historical perspective. We are not sure what will prove significant and what illusory or transitory. But there can be no doubt that this is a new and very different stage in international relations. The world has once again been drastically reduced in size. Almost any statistic regarding international relations shows another huge jump upward. There has been a continued rapid acceleration of the speed at which the world is shrinking, while international relations are growing ever more massive and complex. It seems inevitable that changes over the next few decades will be far greater than the changes that have taken place during the past few decades.

It took many millenniums for mankind to move from the almost completely self-contained and isolated tiny groupings of paleolithic times to the limited indirect trade and cultural contacts of the period of the great classic empires. In the next millennium, man moved through the periods of contact by means of the nomadic peoples and early oceanic commerce to the great breakthrough of an incipient "one world" around 1500. It took less than four centuries from then to the next breakthrough of apparent world unity through Western domination in the second half of the nineteenth century. The next phase of World War I, the League of Nations, and the world depression was a mere matter of decades. And the new phase since World War II is moving even faster.

If charted on graph paper, the history of the emerging "one world" would show the same bold upward-sweeping curve that seems to characterize most measurable human affairs. Whether it be population, economic production, energy consumption, the constructive and destructive power at human command, the volume of world trade, or the speed and frequency of other sorts of communication between the various parts of the world, we find the same basic pattern of growth. This is not surprising, because they are all interrelated phenomena. There was a slow, almost imperceptible creep upward over the early milleniums, a decidedly more rapid rise in recent centuries, still faster growth in recent decades, and a headlong pace today, apparently headed almost straight toward an entirely impossible infinity.

The human race, once scattered thinly around the globe in small groups with little or no contact with one another, is rapidly becoming some sort of vast world community. No one can predict what the world will be like even ten years from now, much less a generation or two hence. But clearly, if civilization and mankind still exist, we will have a vastly more complex, more interrelated, and more interdependent world—in other words, a viable "one world"—or else probably no world at all as far as human beings are concerned.

2 ⊜ THE BALANCE OF POWER

In thinking about international relations, most people focus their chief attention on military defense and the balance of power. In a rapidly shrinking world in which destructive power is growing ever more awesome, this emphasis is not surprising. It is even more understandable when one considers the historical record. In this century we have already suffered two terrible world wars, and, since the end of the second, the United States has experienced two other costly, even if limited, wars. Behind this recent dismal record lie ages of almost incessant fighting between the various tribes, nations, and empires of the world. After countless generations of conditioning of this sort, it is small wonder that people tend to view military defense and the balance of power as the crucial factors that will determine the fate of the world.

Nuclear weapons, of course, have made military matters seem all the more threatening to the future of our nation and the whole human race. The usual picture of a world disaster is of the "other side" developing so great a nuclear advantage that it subjugates "our side," or else that a nuclear holocaust, resulting from the military unpreparedness of "our side" or the miscalculations of the other, wipes out civilization and perhaps all humanity. It is because of such anxieties that both the United States and the Soviet Union devote not far from a tenth of their total wealth to military matters. This is incomparably more than they spend on all the other aspects of international relations combined. Even their foreign trade, which in any case both nations see not so much as a contribution to international relations as a necessary element in their domestic economic lives, falls short of this figure.

No one should dismiss the possibility that a nuclear war might break out between the great powers and destroy civilization. In the present state of mutual distrust between them, it is all but inevitable that the great powers will continue to devote tremendous energy to military defense and concentrate their attention on maintaining what history seems to show is at best a precarious balance of power in the world. At the same time, however, one should bear in mind that there may be other problems which, though less clearly defined, could in the long run prove both more difficult to handle than the relatively clear-cut military issue and even more important in deciding mankind's fate. It would be the height of folly if we concentrated so heavily on the military aspect of international relations that we paid too little attention to these other problems.

We face a very basic question in attempting to judge the relative weight of military and other problems in international relations and the degree of emphasis to be given to each. If military defense and the balance of power are indeed the only or even the major international problems, then a sensible educational response might be simply to concentrate on mathematical and scientific studies, as the United States did during the *sputnik* fright a little over a decade ago, when the Soviet Union was reported to be getting ahead of us in scientific skills and nuclear technology. But if there are other problems that are equally or even more important and complex, then an entirely different educational approach may be called for.

Military power and warfare have, of course, played a major part in shaping history, and a balance of power between nations has been an important method of preserving peace at various times in the past. In my judgment, however, these are dwindling aspects of international relations, while other matters are beginning to loom as more crucial. Limited regional wars will no doubt continue to be fought in the less developed parts of the world, but wars between the great powers appear to be a receding threat. If this is true, then our present heavy concentration on military matters is a somewhat outdated response that runs the danger of diverting our attention and efforts from more serious problems. To test this judgment, we might consider more fully what the military balance of power has meant in the past and what it seems to be today.

The concept of preserving the peace through a balance of power between a number of states is not unique to the Western world. Balance of power politics existed at a sophisticated level among the multiple states of North China in the first millennium B.C., before the founding of the Chinese Empire in the third century of that era. However, the balance of power pattern that absorbs the minds of military strategists today has been derived basically from the experiences of modern Europe, especially in the eighteenth and nineteenth centuries.* At that time there existed in Europe a limited number of major countries, usually around five, which were of somewhat comparable nature and strength. Occasionally, these states resorted to warfare to settle clashes of interest and pride, if one or another thought it had an adequate military advantage. They sought, however, to minimize these conflicts by joining together in various combinations to form two groupings which were of sufficiently equal strength to discourage either side from starting a war.

The lesser European countries existed somewhat precariously between these power alliances, finding their security in the stalemate between them or, as happened to Poland, being gobbled up through their agreements. Because of the tremendous discrepancy between European military power and that of the rest of the world at this particular time in history, the European pattern of balance of power spread to embrace much of the world. India was part of the booty that went to the British, who played the power game most successfully; Africa, like Poland, was divided up among the contenders; but Siam —as Thailand was then called—was preserved as a buffer state between British and French zones in Southeast Asia, much like a neutral Belgium in Europe. This was the

---

* Much of the remainder of this chapter is based on my essay "World Power" that first appeared in *Collier's 1973 Year Book, Covering the Events of 1972*. Copyright © Crowell-Collier Educational Corporation, 1972 (Macmillan Educational Corporation).

traditional balance of power, and it is some modern equivalent of this pattern that people have in mind when they speak of the balance of power in the world today.

For a number of years after World War II a simple bipolar balance seemed to be an adequate description of the situation. There were clearly two miiltary giants—the United States and the Soviet Union—each roughly in balance with the other, and many of the other military powers of any actual or potential significance, such as China, Japan, and the nations of Western and Eastern Europe, were closely allied to one or the other of these superpowers, creating thus two great military blocs in uneasy balance with each other. The rest of the nations —sometimes called the "third world"—were seen as strung out between the two power blocs, as if all were sitting on the same seesaw. They were considered to be leaning to one side or the other or else maintaining a position of precarious neutrality directly between the two at their point of balance. Any movement in this one-dimensional model could only be away from one pole and toward the other. Thus any shift by any nation was seen as potentially upsetting to the world balance of power and therefore as justifying huge military involvements even in such remote and seemingly unimportant areas as Vietnam.

This perception of the world has been shattered in recent years. The split between China and the Soviet Union, which happened more than a decade ago, ruined the basic unilinear model, though Americans continued to cling to it for a long time, as though one end of the seesaw now balanced two boards on the other side. In time it also became obvious that much of the world's population and many of its states were not on the seesaw at all. Some had asserted this all along by calling themselves "nonaligned nations." Others, while accepting alignment, clearly added little or no weight to the side to which they belonged, and in fact, by being a drain on their patron, probably lessened its weight. Thus, much of the world was not in any real sense part of the Soviet-American balancing act. Most peoples were just going their own way, very little affected by the so-called balance of power in the world.

The Sino-Soviet split gave rise for a while to a triangular model, and China was commonly referred to as the third superpower. But there never was much reality to this picture either. Unlike the historical European model, the units were extremely dissimilar and in any case did not pair up in shifting alliances to maintain the supposed balance. The United States and the Soviet Union were both global military powers still in relative balance with each other. China, which by comparison had a backward and weak economy, was only a regional military power. Its large ground forces made it a formidable opponent in conventional warfare on its own or adjacent territory. But unlike the other two, it had little capacity to project its military power at any great distance. Even its start toward nuclear power was more a matter of future possibilities than present realities. It had an extremely long way to go to become a credible menace to either of the real superpowers, and, given their long head start and much greater economic bases, it seemed unlikely that, if China seriously tried to challenge them in nuclear strength, they would slow down enough to permit it to catch up. Contrary to common assumptions, its limited nuclear power also did not give it a capacity for blackmail against its non-nuclear neighbors. Nuclear blackmail to be effective has to be backed up by a credible nuclear threat, which in turn has to be based on a credible capacity to stand up to the great nuclear powers, for they obviously would not stand idly by, permitting nuclear blackmail by China to go unchallenged. The global balance of power thus was not really triangular, nor did the triangular model incorporate the greater part of the world any more successfully than did the bipolar model.

More recently a five-power model, including Western Europe and Japan, has been proposed to explain the rather sudden fluidity in international relations that became apparent in 1971 and 1972. This model, however, seems no more valid than the triangular one. It, too, leaves much of the world virtually unaffected by the supposed balance between the great powers, and it also suffers from a serious asymmetry between the sizes, natures, and relations of the five so-called world powers. China still remains only a regional military power, and Western Europe and Japan are even less comparable to the United States and the Soviet Union in military terms, the one because it is a conglomeration of states with little unified military purpose, the other since its military power is for the most part only a potentiality that is not likely to be realized in the foreseeable future because of the Japanese public's strong aversion to war and militarism.

This asymmetry also exists in other fields besides the military, but in different patterns. China, which has a massive population but a still largely preindustrial economy, is in no sense an economic power comparable to the other four, which are indeed the four major concentrations of economic strength in the world. In organization and relationships, the United States, Western Europe, and Japan form a closely knit triumvirate of highly prosperous global traders, with political institutions based on democracy, economies permitting a relatively high degree of free enterprise, and tremendous and very intimate economic and cultural contacts with one another. The Soviet Union and China, by contrast, are essentially self-contained and isolated societies, with a minimum of contacts with each other or with the other three units. Such characteristics are not just accidental temporary phenomena but are the natural product of their authoritarian societies and their ideal of a controlled, self-sufficient economy.

Given these disparities in military power, social and political organization, and economic and cultural relationships, the traditional concept of a balance of power maintained through shifting alliances among a group of basically similar major players becomes completely inapplicable. The United States, Western Europe, and Japan have a richness of relationships and a depth of shared interests that are unimaginable between any of them and the Soviet Union or China or between the latter two. In other words, the relations which exist between the first three could not conceivably be traded for relations between any one of them and either the Soviet Union or China. To cite one simple example, trade between the United States and Japan will probably continue to be between five and ten times as great as trade between Japan and China and some ten or more times larger than trade between the United States and China.

The bipolar, triangular, and five-power balance of power models are all so unsatisfactory that one is forced to wonder if the whole concept of a worldwide balance of power has much validity. No one would deny the rough nuclear balance between the Soviet Union and the United States; but beyond that, the concept suffers from several serious defects, particularly if one has the European prototype in mind. We have already seen that the so-called great powers and their relations with one another are not even roughly symmetrical and that they therefore are not interchangeable players, as in the traditional model. But there are other even more serious flaws in the concept, which make it probably more confusing than helpful in analyzing the present situation in the world.

The historical European balance of power was a very precarious one, not so much because the players might change sides as because war was a readily accepted alternative to peace. A miscalculation that led to defeat rather than victory would, of course, be painful to a state's pride and might do it some material injury, but the actual damage was far less than that suffered even by the victors in World Wars I and II and incomparably less than what a so-called victor would undergo in a nuclear war today. As a consequence, the major powers of that time were ready to go to war for reasons that would now be considered inconsequential or even frivolous and on the basis of only a slight margin of supposed military advantage. In other words, the balance was an extremely delicate one, as easily upset as a fine scale.

This is hardly the situation today between the major military powers. At the present stage of technological advancement, a third world war would all too likely mean the end of higher civilization—conceivably even the end of the human race. War between the two great nuclear nations would amount to a sort of double suicide. War even at the subnuclear level between any of the actual or potential major military powers would be so devastatingly costly to both contestants and would run such dangers of triggering a nuclear holocaust that all of them would certainly do their best to avoid even this sort of limited warfare. Unlike the European situation in the eighteenth and nineteenth centuries, war between the major military powers can no longer be considered by any of them to be a really acceptable alternative to peace and could be seriously contemplated only under the most dire or unusual circumstances. Thus, the balance of power between them is very solid, more like that of a mountain than a seesaw. It would take some very great shift of forces—something very much out of the ordinary, comparable to a cataclysmic flood or earthquake—to destabilize the balance and set a great landslide of war in motion.

This is not to say that there is no longer any danger of war between the great powers. There are a number of ways in which one might break out. A serious failure in communication, such as a drastic misunderstanding of what a rival power was doing or intended to do, could trigger a war. "Hot lines" and other facilities for rapid communication have been established between some of them in the hope of preventing such mistakes. Or again, a limited confrontation between two or more of the great powers could, through successive miscalculations of the other side's attitudes and responses, escalate to a general confrontation and eventually to all-out war. It is for this reason that, as compared with European states of the eighteenth and nineteenth centuries, the major powers show great restraint in deed, if not in word, when dealing with one another even in relatively minor conflicts of interest or viewpoint.

Another possibility would be that one of the two great nuclear powers established such an overwhelming lead over the other that it became capable of a pre-emptive first strike that could eliminate the capacity of the other to retaliate. This, however, seems very unlikely, and recent SALT agreements between the United States and the Soviet Union, which were designed to limit nuclear defense in particular, appear to be a conscious effort on both sides to prevent such a situation from developing by leaving each side relatively undefended against a nuclear counterattack. One could also imagine war occurring if one of the two great powers went to pieces internally and became incapable of a nuclear response, but again this seems improbable. A more realistic danger might be a proliferation of nuclear weaponry among a large number of nations and the creation of a situation in which a nuclear free-for-all might arise from a nuclear attack of undetermined origin, possibly from some relatively minor power.

These and other possibilities are contingencies that must be guarded against, but they are all extraordinary situations outside the usual meaning of the balance of power. War, instead of being a normal and constantly available alternative to peace between the great powers, has become only a nightmare possibility that all seek to avoid. Because of the massive ties and closely shared interests between the United States, Japan, and the various countries of Western Europe, war between these warmongers of the recent past now seems out of the question. War between these three and either the Soviet Union or China may be more possible but is nonetheless very unlikely. Only between China and the Soviet Union does war seem a real possibility, and that only because the two, being authoritarian states relatively impervious to the pressures of public opinion, could more easily keep a conflict limited to a tolerable level, as in the small border wars in 1938 and 1939 between the Soviet Union and a then authoritarian Japan.

It is the realization of this relative stability of the balance between the great powers, rather than instability or the possible shifting of alliances, that accounts for the present fluidity in big power relationships. When the bipolar model was accepted as a true picture of power realities, any weakening of alliances or rapprochement of erstwhile enemies was viewed with the greatest alarm. Now all the great powers are much less restrained in their dealings with one another. The Japanese feel less dependence on their defense alliance with the United States and move more freely in developing relations with the Soviet Union and China. The United States views with equanimity the broadening of relationships between Western Europe and the Soviet Union and between Japan and China, while itself seeking closer understandings with the Soviet Union and a rapprochement with China in the hope of increasing American leverage in negotiations with Moscow.

The shift away from the bipolar or triangular perceptions of the world situation occurred slowly over a number of years but became suddenly obvious with the first major steps in the Sino-American rapprochement in 1971 and 1972. The spectacular way in which these steps were taken and the sharp increase in other moves between the great powers which followed gave rise to the feeling that a major shift in the balance of power was taking place, but any attempt to interpret these moves in balance of power terms is to misunderstand them entirely.

The various balance of power models are even more misleading when applied to the areas outside the five so-called great powers. In the course of the nineteenth century, virtually the whole world became caught up in the European balance of power, but today most nations follow courses influenced only peripherally, if at all, by notions of balance of power between the major nations.

There are of course exceptions. Poland, Czechoslovakia, and most of the other states of Eastern Europe, whether they wish it or not, are under the military shadow of the Soviet Union and part of its defense system. As industrialized areas close to the heartland of Soviet power, they are relatively susceptible to Soviet control, since Soviet military power is close at hand and their industrialized economies can be more easily manipulated or destroyed than the simpler economies nearer subsistence levels in the less developed countries. They are therefore likely to remain part of whatever balance of power situation the Soviet Union envisions for itself. The client states of the

United States in East Asia, which are classed as its military allies—such as South Korea, Taiwan, Thailand, and the Philippines—have in the past been seen by the United States and by themselves as part of the American balance of power position, but this appears to be changing as the lessons of the Vietnam War sink in. These states stand obviously in a very different relationship to the United States geographically, strategically, and in terms of possibilities of effective control than do the East European states to the Soviet Union.

The position of such countries as Austria, Switzerland, Sweden, Finland, and Yugoslavia between the NATO and Soviet defense blocs in Europe does bear some superficial resemblance to that of the small countries in the traditional European balance of power, though progressively less so as the possibility of major warfare recedes. The Arab-Israeli conflict may be even closer to the nineteenth-century situation. The two superpowers are involved—the one through old ambitions for power in the Mediterranean area and more recent hopes for influence over the Arab world, the other because of the natural sympathies for Israel on the part of Jews in the United States. But in most parts of the world, the supposed balance of power between the great nations has little effect, except to give the other countries the hope that they can utilize great power rivalries to extract more aid or other concessions from one great power or another or possibly from all of them.

The Korean War two decades ago was seen in purely balance of power terms, but the Vietnam War showed the strict limitations of the concept. A balance of power viewpoint did account for the original American involvement, but the United States carefully limited its military efforts in order to avoid a military confrontation with China; and China and the Soviet Union, while bitterly opposed to American actions in Vietnam, were careful to avoid military involvement themselves. When we at last realized that the world balance of power was not really involved in Vietnam, we started our military disengagement from the country. Our final withdrawal we negotiated purely between ourselves and the various Vietnamese groups, not with the other great powers. As of this writing, the eventual outcome in Indochina still remains uncertain, but it clearly will be something that is determined basically by the inhabitants of that area, not by big power agreements forced on them against their will, as probably would have been the case in the nineteenth century.

The point is further illustrated by the hands-off policy of the big powers in the wars and general slaughterings of ethnic or political enemies that have gone on in such countries as the Congo (now called Zaire), Indonesia, and Nigeria. An even better illustration was the war at the end of 1971 between India and Pakistan, which resulted in the birth of the nation of Bangladesh—the eighth most populous country in the world. This upheaval in the Indian subcontinent, which involved almost a fifth of the world's population, did produce sharp reactions from the United States, China, and the Soviet Union, the first two siding against the third; but their threats and alarms amounted to little more than posturings. They had little if any effect on the outcome, which was determined by the people on the spot. Clearly, whatever balance of power exists between the great powers affects the rest of the world but slightly.

Here we see another great difference between the present world situation and that of the worldwide balance of power in the nineteenth century, when at relatively little cost the great powers could determine the fate of most of the rest of the world and divide it up between them. The reason for this change seems basically to be the rise of nationalism throughout the world. The gap in technological skills and economic power between the less developed countries and the great industrialized nations has continued to widen, and the latter have vastly increased their capacity to extend their military might great distances. The rapid rise of nationalism in the less developed countries, however, has more than offset these growing advantages of the great powers. It has made it possible for the less developed countries to frustrate efforts at military and political domination by more powerful but distant nations. In the nineteenth century, it was taken for granted that small modernized military forces backed by a little bit of naval power could defeat much larger armies that lacked the backbone of nationalism. Today, nationally aroused populations in technologically backward areas can retreat with relative ease into a subsistence economy and then, through guerrilla warfare and civil resistance, make foreign efforts at control either impossible or at least too costly to be worthwhile.

This basic change in the relationship between the great powers and the countries on which they had preyed first became evident in the 1930's and 1940's, when the Chinese, aroused by a new nationalism, frustrated Japan's determined efforts at conquest. It was again demonstrated after World War II in the failure of the Dutch to recover control over Indonesia and the French to maintain control over Indochina and Algeria. The rapid dismantling of overseas empires throughout the world at that time was tacit recognition of the change that had taken place. The Vietnam War illustrated it once again in a particularly clear and tragic form. The United States, the strongest of all the world powers, making efforts absurdly disproportionate to the size of Vietnam or the importance of the issues at stake, could wreak havoc throughout the country but could not achieve the objectives it sought in the war.

One by-product of this changed power relationship between the great nations and the less developed countries is a further lessening of the likelihood of armed conflict between the great powers. In the heyday of the European balance of power, rivalries over trade and political control in the less developed regions of the world were major reasons for wars. The great powers constantly came into conflict over markets for their manufactured goods in these other lands, sources of raw materials, bases for the further extension of military, economic, and political influence, and places where they could fly their respective flags, largely for the sake of national prestige. Most of this is now a thing of the past. Rivalries for markets and raw materials may still exist, but they do not lead to military conflicts, simply because markets and sources of raw materials can no longer be won by war or maintained by colonial control. Open efforts at domination over a less developed country are likely to prove prohibitively costly and end up in the economic expulsion of the great power. Now that the "third world" is no longer seen as part of a bipolar world balance, it seems improbable that there will be further serious big power conflicts over these areas or military involvements by any of the great powers on a scale at all comparable to the intervention of the United States in Vietnam.

The stability in the balance between the great powers and their military disengagement from the less developed nations, however, do not mean that the latter too will enjoy stability and peace. They are almost by definition relatively unstable countries. Their human skills, economies, and social and political institutions are inadequately developed. Many of them are newly created units, sometimes with rather arbitrary boundaries and still unsettled relations with their neighbors. Many no doubt will suffer internal disruptions, and some may be afflicted by war.

In a sense it is only the less developed countries that can afford warfare today, because war is much less likely to lead to total destruction for them than for the great industrialized nations. It is therefore a more acceptable alternative to peace. Such local conflicts and disturbances, however, will probably not affect relations between the great powers or be much influenced by their relationships. A local balance of power, as between Vietnam, Cambodia, and Thailand, or between India, Pakistan, and Bangladesh, may have some meaning for the region affected, but not for the relations between the great powers or for world peace overall.

Thus, for a number of reasons, traditional balance of power concepts do not have much relevance today. I have gone into this subject in some detail because it is important for us to realize that our attention and efforts in international relations have been seriously misdirected. The basic point I am trying to make is that the present world situation has evolved far away from that of the eighteenth and nineteenth centuries, or even the first half of the twentieth, when the great bulk of the relations between nations had to do with the possibilities and realities of war. Despite the overwhelming attention we still pay to military defense and balance of power politics, these should no longer be the major concerns in international relations, at least for the more industrialized countries. During the past few decades, war has shrunk from being a dangerous but exciting probability to the status of a horrible but only peripheral possibility. In the meantime, other international problems have risen to take its place as the chief threats to mankind's future. We should concentrate our attention on these, attempting to discern not just what they are today but how they are likely to develop over the decades ahead.

3 ☙ LOOMING WORLD PROBLEMS

No one can predict what precise form problems of international relations will take during the next generation or two. It is hard enough to analyze and reach agreement about those that we already face. But certain directions of development are clear and do suggest where some of the major problem areas may lie.

One certainly will be the precarious balance between man and the natural resources on which he depends. This is an old story. Time after time the population of certain areas has outrun local productivity, with the result that starvation or disorders stopped further growth and in some cases brought about a serious decline in the whole level of economic activity and political and social organization. Because of this historical record, Robert Malthus in 1798 propounded the general rule that population tends to outpace food supply, usually with disastrous consequences.

Few people today subscribe to the Malthusian theory in its original form. He failed to take adequate account of advances in agricultural technology and transportation that would vastly increase food production in most parts of the world and make surpluses in one area available for consumption in another. Despite the enormously increased population of the world since his day, his gloomy theory has proved in modern times a receding fear. For the foreseeable future, world food resources will probably stay ahead of total population. We have recently seen the development of "miracle" wheat and rice strains, and other agricultural breakthroughs no doubt will follow. The pressures on world food supplies may also be relieved by a number of other still somewhat remote but entirely conceivable technological advances, such as the scientific "farming" of the oceans or the desalination of sea water to make coastal deserts bloom like the rose.

We should not dismiss Malthus too quickly, however. The bulk of the world's population still lives in hunger, not far above starvation levels. Breakdowns in the distribution system because of warfare or political or economic inefficiency still produce famines in some areas. And the whole balance between people and food exists at a much higher statistical level than in the past and continues to rise rapidly.

The world's population at present stands roughly halfway between 3 and 4 billion—about four times its size in Malthus's day—and it is doubling about every thirty-five years. At this rate it could reach 7 billion early in the twenty-first century, 14 billion by 2040, and close to 50 billion by the end of the century. If population growth continues indefinitely at its present speed, stark Malthusian limits will obviously be reached sooner or later, and in any case it seems altogether improbable that a decent and worthwhile standard of life could exist for anybody if such masses of humanity swarmed over the globe. Men would have reduced themselves to the level of the lemmings.

The problem is compounded by the fact that the bulk of population growth is occurring, not in the areas of abundant food resources, but in the areas of food deficiency. The advanced industrialized nations, which also include the chief areas of agricultural surplus, average around 1 per cent in population growth per year—a rate that causes them little or no problem—and some of them show signs of achieving zero population growth. In the poorer countries, however, population increases average close to 2½ per cent—a dangerously high figure. In some countries they reach as high as 3½ per cent. Indeed, there seems to be a direct causal link between poverty and high population growth. Poverty actually may be the only important causal factor, except for the worldwide improvement of hygiene, which has meant that high birth rates now result in much greater rates of population growth than they once did.

Since poverty is receding only very slowly in most of the world, it seems likely that high rates of population growth will continue for some time. It is true that in China the government, primarily through a system of late marriages, seems to have brought down the growth rate to about 1½ per cent, but China is exceptional among the less developed countries in being tightly organized and having a long tradition of firm political and social controls. In most other parts of the world, rates of population growth have fallen only after industrialization has produced a high degree of urbanization and affluence. Since a rapidly rising population eats up economic growth, leaving little or no gain in per capita terms, most of the less developed countries are caught in a vicious circle, or one might call it a perilous race between population and prosperity. To the extent that their increases in population offset their economic growth, they will not achieve a level of industrialization and wealth sufficient to cut significantly into their birth rates and thus dissolve permanently the Malthusian menace.

In the long run a leveling off of the world's population will be absolutely necessary, but for the foreseeable future it seems probable that it will continue to grow swiftly and that the imbalance will increase between the areas of surplus production and the areas with surplus mouths to feed. To compensate for such conditions, there must be not only a steady rise in agricultural technology but also increasing cooperation and skill in the distribution of food internationally as well as within the national units. Malthus only had in mind local conditions of relatively low population density and growth as well as low food productivity. In the historical record he knew, the balance had never got very far above the levels of a relatively primitive subsistence agriculture. Today, with population at incomparably higher levels and the balance involving worldwide rather than merely local factors, it can only be maintained by far greater technical skills and broader and much more complex networks of cooperation. Moreover, the needs go on multiplying rapidly. The higher the level of balance between people and food, the worse a breakdown of that balance would be. As compared with the days of Malthus, it might be like the difference between a fall from a high-rise apartment and from the backyard fence. Thus even the classic problem of food has not been entirely dispelled.

I have discussed food resources first, because hunger and famine have always loomed so large in the human experience; but shortages in other resources are likely to prove a more seriously limiting factor to human growth and a more probable cause of dangerous breakdown. The rapidly accelerating speed of industrialization has completely transformed the world that Malthus knew. The consumption of metals and the fossil fuels of oil, gas, and coal for the production of energy has shot up and is still rising at an astronomic rate. The total production of energy comes close to doubling every decade, while the consumption of oil and gas more than doubles. Most of this huge rise in consumption has been in the industrialized nations, resulting from rapid economic growth in some of them, such as Japan and West Germany, and substantial technological advances in all. Less than a third of the people of the world live in these countries, but they alone threaten to put serious pressures on the world's mineral resources within the next few decades. The more than two-thirds of the world's population in the still largely preindustrial countries is certain to increase its consumption of these resources, too, and if the less developed countries were to industrialize rapidly enough to put a curb on their population growth before the total world population reaches unmanageable levels, then the pressure on these resources will increase at a still more alarming rate. We face a mind-boggling dilemma between a too slow rate of industrialization in the less developed

countries that sets off a slow-ticking population bomb and a run on the world bank of natural resources that bankrupts us all.

We should not, however, draw too simple and stark a picture, as is done all too frequently. Take oil, for example, as one of the most crucial natural resources in possibly short supply. It is easy to point out that at present rates of rapidly increasing consumption, the known exploitable oil resources of the world will be exhausted within a fairly short span of time. But such a prediction ignores the discovery of new resources, the development of new techniques for tapping presently unexploitable resources, and the appearance of new technology that shifts the burden for producing energy from oil to other resources, such as electric energy produced by nuclear power, the tides, or even by direct solar energy. These and other variables make any straight-line projection undoubtedly false and any specific prediction dubious. It is for this reason that the various efforts at drawing a clear quantitative picture of the problem are always met by a chorus of refutations that point out the variables likely to ameliorate the situation. Of course, there are also likely to be unforeseen variables that will make it worse. But, whatever the specifics may prove to be, there are enough storm clouds on the horizon to give rise to serious worries about the worldwide balance between rising population and per capita consumption on the one side and the natural resources available to mankind on the other.

Closely associated with this problem is the danger of worldwide pollution and ecological breakdown, a problem that has been widely perceived only in recent years. The transformation of natural resources into heat and energy and the unchecked production of noxious industrial wastes have already produced serious local pollution problems in certain areas of industrial and population concentration, particularly in Japan, Western Europe, and the United States. But far more serious than these local problems is the possibility that increasing worldwide industrialization might have a drastic effect on the global environment. Pollutants in the air or water, for example, might build up to lethal levels. Chemicals that are not biodegradable, such as DDT and mercury, are spreading throughout the world and threaten to rise to levels that might menace human as well as animal life, even in areas far from the original sources of pollution. A continuation of the present accelerating rate of industrialization might also lead to a heating up of the oceans of the world or might put enough impurities into the atmosphere to affect the penetration of the sun's rays or the retention of atmospheric heat on a scale sufficient to produce catastrophic changes in the world's climate. Again the specifics are by no means certain. No one knows for sure how much effect expanding industrialization will have on the oceans or the atmosphere or how much of a change in the purity and temperature of air and water would result in a dangerous alteration of the climate. The ability of men to mitigate this sort of global pollution by new or more effectively applied technology is even less predictable. What may seem like great dangers today could in the future prove to be entirely controllable technical matters. But, as in the case of natural resources, there are enough clouds gathering on the horizon to give ample reason for concern about the future.

The problems of ecology and natural resources have

drawn much attention in recent years. Innumerable books and pamphlets have been published about their various ramifications. Wise men have gathered in Rome to state one side of the case, and they have been answered by thunderous volleys from other wise men all over the world. These are, of course, extremely complex but also very basic issues that deserve careful study. But not here. Others have treated these subjects with far more knowledge and authority than I could pretend to. In any case, a detailed consideration of these particular problems would divert us from the main thesis of this book. I cite them merely as examples of the increasingly difficult problems that mankind faces, which if not properly handled could lead to the collapse of civilization just as certainly as would an all-out war between the great powers.

The problems of world population, natural resources, and the global environment, I suspect, are only a few among many that may challenge mankind in the decades ahead. They are some of the problems that we, in our limited, time-bound perspective, can now visualize; by the year 2000, others beyond our present imagination will probably have taken shape. But even these few may help to illustrate what would appear to be a common problem underlying them all. In the race between rising technology on the one hand and soaring requirements for natural resources and growing dangers of worldwide pollution on the other, it seems quite possible that technology will stay safely ahead. These problems, however, are not merely matters of adequate scientific knowledge. Since they are global in their effect and require international solutions, they raise the question of man's capacity for adequate worldwide cooperation. Here once again we see how all men are being drawn willy-nilly into a single vast world community.

To make the point more specifically, the citizens of Los Angeles, Rome, and Tokyo will probably in their own interests take measures to stem or even mitigate the disagreeable conditions of local pollution they face, but they cannot be expected to adopt on their own initiative costly technological innovations aimed at lessening global ecological problems or easing the worldwide pressure on natural resources. To do so, when others do not, would be to lessen their competitive economic position in the world. Such steps would require not just national but international agreements, because no country is likely to accept substantial economic sacrifices in comparison with other countries simply for the benefit of mankind as a whole at some time in the future.

As things now stand, it seems much more probable that men will develop the technology to handle the problems they face than that they will be able to work out international agreements to apply this technology successfully. International agreements already exist in a number of fields in which the costs are slight and chaos for everyone would quickly result if there were no agreements—postal, telegraphic, and radio communications, procedures of oceanic and air navigation, trade relations, the control of epidemics, and the like. But there have been few and only extremely hesitant agreements in fields in which the costs of current operations would be considerably increased merely to meet some still distant-seeming menace like global pollution or insufficient natural resources. Men organized into national units seem extraordinarily myopic on such matters. Those who have little or nothing to lose may appear far-sighted and express idealistic concern about the human fate; but those with immediate interests at stake usually prove to be selfishly short-sighted.

A good though trifling illustration is the current international controversy over the catching of whales. Whatever the merits of the respective arguments may be, it is very clear that as the number of nations seriously engaged in whaling shrank to two—Japan and the Soviet Union —most of the other industrialized countries developed a concern that current whaling practices would lead to the extinction of this largest of all mammals. The Japanese and Russians, however, continued to regard such arguments with skepticism and maintained that substantial national economic interests were involved. The whaling crisis is only symptomatic of a much broader problem— the conservation of the resources of the sea as a whole. There is, for example, great danger that international competition in fishing in general will lead to a serious depletion of the world's fish resources and thus to plummeting yields. The resultant rise in prices would mean that what fish were caught would go to the richer countries, with a consequent decline in the availability of this important source of protein in the countries that are already dangerously low in protein consumption.

Even the highly interdependent community of industrialized, trading nations that centers on Western Europe, North America, and Japan has shown no great capacity for cooperation on matters that involve significant national economic costs. The ability of these countries to cooperate with the Soviet Union and the other industrialized Communist nations of Eastern Europe appears to be even less. But the greatest problem is likely to be that of cooperation between the industrialized nations and the bulk of humanity in the still largely preindustrial countries.

The perspective on such global problems is very different between these two groups. For example, the people of the industrialized nations, being the chief consumers of the world's resources and its main polluters, will probably become seriously concerned about such problems long before those in the less developed countries are aroused to the danger. It is only natural that to the people of the poorer countries their own rapid industrialization seems much more important than still unrealized and not entirely certain threats to the natural resources of the world and the global environment. A good example of this difference in viewpoints was seen a few years ago in the effort of some of the industrialized countries to persuade the less developed ones to join them in a ban on DDT. The poorer nations flatly refused, since DDT seemed to them essential for the control of malaria and pests that threatened their already inadequate food supplies. These were immediate and vital interests, not hypothetical problems of the future.

The people of the poorer countries tend to feel that all such problems of pollution and natural resources are matters that only the already affluent nations can afford to worry about. After all, Americans, Europeans, and Japanese on a per capita basis are polluting the world and using up its resources at a rate anywhere from 10 to 50 times higher than the citizens of the less developed nations. The latter are likely to feel that they need have no worry about such matters until they are consuming and polluting at a comparable rate—by which time, of course, it may be too late. Exhortations to put a brake on unbridled industrialization in the interests of global ecology and the preservation of resources may seem to them an effort on the part of the industrialized nations to maintain their lead, just as talk about birth control is often considered to be a racist effort to preserve the resources of the world for the already rich nations.

If the threat of global pollution and of a dangerous imbalance between population, economic growth, and natural resources continues to materialize, I have little doubt that men throughout the world will eventually begin to take these problems to heart, but the real question is whether they will do so soon enough to take effective action and whether, even when aroused, they will show the skill in international relations needed to handle these problems adequately. These seem to me the real dangers, rather than a lack of technology. A fatal delay or inadequacy of the response could come at any one of three points of convergence—or possibly at all three—in the relations within the present interdependent world community of Western Europe, North America, and Japan, between this community and the industrialized Communist states, or between both of these and the developing nations. The last would appear to be the most likely stage for disastrous failure.

Worries about world resources and pollution are premised in part on the assumption that the less developed nations, through industrialization, will eventually join the more affluent countries as major consumers of natural resources and destroyers of the global environment. If that does not happen, these particular pressures will be eased, but two possibly greater threats might then materialize. One, as we have already seen, would be the unabated multiplication of total population because of continuing poverty in most of the world. This course leads to perhaps delayed but still inevitable catastrophe. But probably before that ultimate Malthusian tragedy unfolds, another disaster will have intervened.

The less than one-third of the world's population in the Communist as well as non-Communist industrialized nations accounts for some five-sixths of the world's production, while the remaining more than two-thirds of the human race has only a pathetic sixth of the total. Since the industrialized nations are on the whole growing faster economically than the less developed lands, this tremendous economic gap between the two is widening steadily. When one factors in the more rapid rate of population growth in the preindustrial countries, the per capita well-being of the two groups can be seen to be diverging even more rapidly. Already the measurable income of an average inhabitant of the Indian subcontinent or of sub-Sahara Africa is less than one-twentieth of that of an average Japanese and only about one-fortieth of that of an American.

If the gap between the poor and the rich nations continues to widen for very long into the future, then the prospects for a viable world in the twenty-first century grow decidedly dimmer. Tensions between the South and the North, as the two groups of countries are commonly called, might well increase to explosive proportions. We see hints of this already in the fierce resentments the less developed countries show toward the richer and more powerful ones and in the very different perspectives the two groups have on the problems of ecology and natural resources. If such strains continue to increase, then a global political breakdown might well overwhelm civilization even before it is crushed by its overburden of population.

It cannot be denied that great discrepancies in economic well-being between different regions of the world have existed for thousands of years without causing major problems for mankind, but this was because a single world community was as yet quite unimaginable. Even a century and a half ago, people in India and the United States or in China and Europe had little more influence on each other's lives than did, say, the ancient Egyptians and Chinese. But this is no longer true, even though the contrasts in wealth have grown much greater in the meantime. As we have seen, all forms of international relationships and interdependence are increasing at a rapidly accelerating speed. What this may mean for mankind can be illustrated by drawing an analogy with domestic conditions in the United States.

A mere century ago the newly freed blacks in our society were frozen into the position of being only second-class citizens. Other groups too fell into this general category. But our society remained vigorous and healthy. The discrepancies between the underprivileged minorities and the bulk of the citizens raised serious problems only in parts of the land and in limited aspects of its life. However, as technological advances drew the nation more closely together and made the relations between different aspects of its life more complex, such discrepancies raised increasing problems, until dangerous tensions developed. Wide differences in privilege and opportunity between different groupings in our heterogeneous society came to threaten its very viability. And this despite the fact that the actual gap in privilege and opportunity had been starting to close in recent decades. Today, it is not enough simply to ameliorate the attitudes and practices which seemed adequate in the nineteenth century. More basic, even revolutionary, changes are proving necessary for the more complex, more closely interrelated age in which we now live.

The world, of course, may be drawing together as a highly interrelated, interdependent unit more slowly than the United States did. The distances are greater and the separateness of the subunits more distinct. But, as we have seen, technology is having the same basic effect worldwide that it had in our country. The direction of motion and the acceleration of the speed of change are the same. What differences do exist between the world situation and that within the United States are more frightening than comforting. In the world it is the large majority, not the minority, that is underprivileged, and the gap is widening rather than shrinking.

This problem, I believe, could very well reach such explosive proportions that it will threaten the viability of all civilization. I would not attempt to predict just how such a situation might come about. Americans of 1900 or even of 1928 would have had great difficulty in foretelling the course of racial and social ferment of the 1960's and the 1970's. We would probably do no better today in predicting the specific world problems of the year 2000. But we can dimly perceive at least some of the looming dangers.

I have argued that the instabilities of the less developed areas do not today exert much influence on the balance of power between the great powers, but this is not to say that a growing imbalance between islands of prosperity and wide areas of poverty and disorder would not have a deleterious effect on the health of the whole world. The impact of such a situation would certainly become more and more serious the further technology advances. Without doubt the space between the nations of the world will continue to shrink, their contacts to multiply, and the complexities of their relationships to grow—and all at an accelerating rate. Power, too, will increase greatly—for destructive as well as constructive purposes.

I have suggested that the proliferation of nuclear weapons might be one path to an armageddon that destroys us all. It seems quite probable that other forms of terribly destructive power—germ warfare, for example—may be available even to relatively poor and backward nations in the twenty-first century. Clearly, worldwide capacities for disruption and destruction are growing much faster than is the economic well-being of the less developed countries. Imagine the threat to civilization if the bulk of the world's population continues to be dissatisfied and resentful, not feeling a sense of participation in the world community and despairing of ever starting to close the gap with the more advanced nations, much less achieving real equality. What hope for human survival would we have then? One can perhaps get some inkling of the insecurities of such an advanced but precarious age from the rash of airplane hijackings and the murderous disruption of the 1972 Olympic Games in Munich.

It might be pointed out that some of these possible threats to the viability of the world lie in the military field, which I have discounted as a major area of danger. This is quite true, but these threats are not basically military in origin. A military explosion might be the fatal symptom of the disease, but its basic causes would more probably be the growing economic gap in the world and behind this gap the failure to develop adequate international understanding and cooperation to cope with the problem. To prepare only for possible military confrontation might make a military explosion almost inevitable.

We may not be able to predict exactly the situation that lies ahead of us, but that does not make the dangers any less real. We cannot prescribe the solutions any more specifically, but at least one thing is clear. Something obviously has to be done, first to stop the gap between the rich and poor countries from widening further, and then to start to close it. Only in this way will the bulk of the world's population be given hope and a sense of self-respecting and meaningful participation in a world community. This again is a problem not so much of technology as of international understanding and skills in cooperation.

Hitherto the chief means of attempting to close the

gap between the rich and poor nations has been "aid," which is the collective name for grants, loans, and investments of the rich, industrialized nations directed toward the less developed countries. The whole concept of aid has recently fallen into disrepute, largely because it has been misunderstood and misused. The false assumption in the early postwar years that aiding the preindustrial countries to develop would be no more difficult than restoring the already industrialized economies of war-torn Western Europe and Japan led to deep disappointment over the efficacy of aid. This was true both in the United States, which contributed so greatly to the recovery of Western Europe and Japan, and in the less developed countries, which had expected to rise industrially like these restored areas.

The misuses of aid programs have also been many. Much of the total aid effort, especially on the part of the United States and the Soviet Union, has been directed toward buying political and military allies in the balance of power game, rather than toward economic and institutional development that would contribute to the closing of the gap. The result has often been support for inefficient or even reactionary régimes and the diversion of grants to military expenditures far beyond the real needs of the country being aided. Loans and investments, especially by Japan and some of the European countries, have commonly been aimed at facilitating the donor country's export program and securing for it the raw materials it needed, rather than toward the long-range development of the recipient countries. The bilateral nature of most aid has also caused political tensions, exacerbated by the attitudes of arrogance and condescension on the part of the donor countries and the prickly pride and resentment of the recipients. Almost inevitably, bilateral aid has raised fears in the less developed countries that it is a stratagem for transforming the blatant political imperialism of recent centuries into a more subtle economic imperialism.

Despite these weaknesses, aid should not be written off as a hoax. It was one of the greatest inventions of the postwar world. In view of the hitherto unbroken history of strong nations ruthlessly preying on weak ones, the United States deserves great credit for leading the way in developing the concept that the rich nations should instead give aid to the poor. If the failings of the aid concept can be corrected, it could play an important, perhaps even a crucial, role in closing the dangerous gap.

Grants should be utilized, not to purchase allies, but for vital development tasks for which other financial sources are not available. Loans and investments should be designed with the needs of the recipients taken fully into consideration, not just the interests of the donors. The level of aid should not be determined by temporary political and strategic considerations but by the needs of the recipient country and its demonstrated ability to use these resources effectively for long-range economic growth and institutional development. Care should be taken to see that the proliferating multi-national corporations play a truly constructive role from the point of view of the developing nations, for these economic giants will probably have a major part, not just in investments, but in the transfer of skills to the developing nations; at present their role is not well understood anywhere and is deeply mistrusted in the poorer countries. The humiliating overtones of the aid relationship for the recipient should be mitigated by making aid multilateral or impersonally international whenever possible, and by much greater tact in bilateral dealings.

Aid while useful, however, will probably never be enough to make the difference between a widening and a closing gap between the rich and poor nations. Much more important will be trade. The problem here is to open markets in the rich countries for the manufactures of the poor ones. Except for the oil-rich lands, especially those in the Middle East with thin populations and huge subsurface riches, the less developed nations will never close the gap just by exporting raw materials and tropical goods to the already industrialized nations. Bananas and coffee are not enough. The less developed nations, too, will have to industrialize. And to do this fast enough and on a large enough scale to get significantly ahead of population growth, they will have to have not just their own small markets for the industrial goods they are able to produce, but some of the really large markets of the world, meaning those in the rich nations.

It would be desirable, for example, for the industrialized nations to import more of the raw materials and foodstuffs they get from the less developed countries in semi-processed form, thus allowing the poor countries to take part a little more in the lucrative manufacturing process. But present trade patterns and policies tend to militate against this happening. It also would be wise for the industrialized nations to reach agreements on preferential tariffs favoring the manufactured goods of the less developed countries or even agreements to shift the purchasing of certain industrial goods from their own domestic producers and those of other advanced nations to the developing countries.

The low-capital, labor-intensive industries are the natural ones for less developed nations to start with. A good example is textiles. It would make sense for the already industrialized nations to phase themselves out of such fields and buy the products of these industries from the less industrialized nations. This would free their own labor, management, and financial resources for more advanced and productive industries, the output of which could then be sold more readily to the less advanced nations as they too started to prosper. In this way their own long-range economic interests would be served, rather than hurt. But the really important point is that the gap might start to close, and thus the prospects for human survival in the twenty-first century would improve a great deal.

Unfortunately, there are few signs that the world is ready to take such steps. Faced with the social and political problems of phasing out industries like textiles and moving those engaged in them to more productive occupations, the United States chooses to follow the uneconomic but politically simpler course of protecting what otherwise would be declining industries. And Japanese and Americans, far from agreeing to purchase more of their textiles from India and the other less developed countries, quarrel bitterly over the small share Japan has in the American market, even though this share is really quite inconsequential in terms of the economy of either nation.

The industrialized countries seem even less ready to take other more painful steps that may prove necessary if a global catastrophe is to be averted. They may simply have to curtail their own consumption of the world's resources, not just to make the supply last longer for themselves, but to make more of it available for the less developed countries of the world as they creep a little closer in living standards and consumption to the world leaders. At the present moment, the hope that the industrialized countries could bring themselves to do this seems almost visionary.

I have touched on only a few aspects of the problem of narrowing the gap between the poor and the rich countries. It has been my purpose not to analyze in detail the difficulties of aid and trade but to show that the real problem is not so much a matter of technology as of international understanding and skills. Here again, as in the other looming global problems I have mentioned, the key question is whether we can develop soon enough a sense of mankind's shared interests and common fate and a capacity to take more effective international action on these problems. A look at mankind's record on such matters in the past is not at all reassuring.

4 ✛ THE EXPANDING UNIT
OF COOPERATION

There can be little doubt that the world is becoming
a single unit for mankind. This is happening whether we
like it or not. It is the inevitable result of human inven-
tiveness. But men are slow in accepting the fact that this
means global interdependence. They are slow in developing the sense of world community that is necessary if a
unitary world is to prove a place where men can live and
civilization survive. As in so much else that we see in
life around us, man's creative power threatens to outpace
his understanding and psychological adaptability. Can he
adjust rapidly enough to survive under the conditions that
he is creating for himself? A glance back at history leaves
reason for doubt. The unit of shared interests and effective cooperation has gradually expanded over the millenniums, but only very slowly and uncertainly.

For hundreds of thousands of years the unit through
which men and their subhuman forbears survived in a
menacing environment was the small, family-like hunting
and gathering band. The transition from such groups to
larger tribal and agricultural communities was probably
made over a period of thousands of years. There was
ample time for people to adjust to the concept that their

community had become this larger unit, embracing perhaps several hundred people, not all of them clearly related by blood to one another, rather than just a score or so of closely related individuals.

The transition to still larger groupings—such as tribal federations, small city states, and the early empires—in which the basic unit of human activity included many thousands of people not in daily contact with one another, probably came a little more rapidly, but even then it was measured in millenniums or at the very least in centuries. Over a number of generations, people could become accustomed to the larger, more impersonal unit of shared interests and cooperation. The sense of community could slowly be expanded to embrace many people beyond the individual's own ken.

In the last millennium of the pre-Christian era, there was a significant breakthrough to much larger, more diverse, and more populous units—that is, the classic empires. The ancient Egyptian Empire had for thousands of years embraced a large population spread the length of the lower Nile River, but it was in size and nature quite different from the Roman Empire, in which it was but one of many parts.

The Roman Empire did not suddenly appear full blown. It too was the product of centuries of evolutionary development. It was foreshadowed by the more transitory Persian and Macedonian empires and had a long history of growth in Italy before it spread throughout the Mediterranean region. The story of the early empires of India is less clear, but in China the historical process was quite similar to that of Rome. The political unit slowly grew over the centuries, and in the late third century B.C., after a brief imperial unification of China's hitherto disparate parts by the Ch'in, the Han established a more lasting imperial system. Thus men had generations in which to become accustomed to the new and much larger imperial unit and to develop a sense of identification with it.

Military technology, such as mass armies made possible by a plentiful supply of iron weapons and more rapid and far-reaching communication by horseback in place of chariots, may have accounted in part for the appearance of the great classic empires. Even more important perhaps was the development of unifying ideas—that is, philosophic and religious concepts of broad appeal, capable of transcending narrow cultural and political boundaries. The growth of Hindu and Buddhist ideas in India probably played a role in the rise of the classic Indian empires. This was certainly true in the case of the Buddhist empire of Asoka, and in the long run Hinduism proved a far greater force for unity in India than did the kaleidoscopic succession of temporal powers. In China, the amalgam of Confucian philosophical concepts with other strains of early Chinese thought seems to have been a major reason for the long success of the Han Empires, and ever since then cultural and philosophical unity has interacted with political centralization to make China the unique example of a classic empire that still persists in the present human geography of the world. In the Mediterranean area and the Middle East, Greek philosophy gave cultural unity for many centuries to the Hellenic world, contrasting sharply in its durability with the brief flicker of political unity under Alexander. Greek thought also, as developed and added to by the Latins, underlay the political unity of the Roman Empire.

As the classical empires foundered, the great philosophic and religious traditions became all the more the major unifying forces in human affairs. Christianity, an offshoot of the remarkable Jewish tradition of the Hebrew prophets as filtered through the minds of men conditioned by Greek thought, became the great unifying force in the dying Roman Empire and came to represent whatever integration the Mediterranean area and Euprope enjoyed in a long age of political fragmentation. Emerging a few centuries later from a Judeo-Christian background, Islam bought a momentary political unity to the Middle East and North Africa and continued to spread until it produced cultural bonds between these regions, Central Asia, and large parts of the Indian subcontinent and Southeast Asia.

Buddhism too spread from India throughout Central Asia, China, Korea, Japan, and most of Southeast Asia. While it produced no world empire like that of early Islam, it appears to have achieved for a while a greater cultural unity over a larger proportion of the human race than ever existed before or since, excepting, of course, the cultural unity, if one can call it that, of today's worldwide secular religion of economic growth and "modernization." Buddhist monuments and sculptures of the seventh to ninth centuries show an amazing uniformity between the temple caves of Ajanta in India, the remains of Buddhist strongholds in the Tarim Basin of Central Asia, the temple caves of North China, the Sokkuram grotto of Korea, the many monasteries that surrounded the old Nara capital of Japan, and the great monument at Borobudur in Java.

The universal philosophies and religions, however,

while serving as more durable unifiers than did the classic empires, suffered the ravages of time, usually warred with one another, and commonly divided into mutually battling sects. Buddhism was disrupted by the inroads of Islam and the resurgence of Hinduism in India and Confucianism in China and Korea, leaving behind only isolated and sharply dissimilar remnants of its once great cultural unity. Islam was never able to re-create its early political unity and became divided into rival doctrines. Christianity spread with the European peoples throughout the Western Hemisphere and Australia, and, like Buddhism and Islam, was extended through missionary zeal to some other peoples; but it achieved no real political unity and became divided into three major lines and many minor sects which fought furiously with one another. Worse still, these various religions engaged in seemingly unending warfare with each other—Christianity with Islam and Islam with Hinduism and Buddhism.

The classic empires and the great world religions thus produced much larger units of mutual interest and cooperation than had existed before, but they achieved these only slowly and imperfectly. Indeed, the great religions, like the political and economic ideologies of today, often served more as divisive than as unifying forces. The classic empires, with the single exception of the Chinese Empire, all disappeared, to be succeeded in time by other similar empires, which proved no more lasting, as in the case of the Mongol, the Ottoman, the Mogul, and the British and French empires.

After the appearance of the classic empires and the great philosophic and religious traditions of the era between the sixth century B.C. and the seventh century A.D., there were no major new developments in the unit of human organization until relatively recent times. Over the past few centuries, however, an apparently stronger and possibly more durable unit has slowly emerged. This is the so-called nation state, which in its most typical form is a fairly large, geographically compact unit, made up of people sharing a common language and culture. The closely interrelated interests of the people of each nation state have come to be seen as overriding those of its geographic, cultural, or economic subunits and as clashing sharply with the interests of other nation states.

The nation state basically grew out of cultural and political developments in Western Europe, as kings slowly established their power over a welter of feudal authorities in late medieval and early modern times, and the loose confederation of Christendom broke up into mutually antagonistic states, most of which corresponded roughly in extent with the area in which some distinctive language, such as English or French, was spoken. Historical developments elsewhere in the world, however, contributed to the spread of the nation state pattern to other regions. The early identification in East Asia of the linguistic and cultural unit with a centralized political authority undoubtedly contributed to the relatively successful adoption of the nation state pattern in that part of the world. The second Han Empire of China fell apart even more rapidly than did Rome but left behind a stronger sense of political unity in a geographically more compact and culturally more homogeneous area. Perhaps for this reason a united Chinese Empire was re-created by the late sixth century, and China remained thereafter essentially a single great linguistic, cultural, and political unit. Probably influenced by this example, the Japanese, too, achieved by the seventh century a clear sense of one people, one language, and one nation, which was to remain vigorously alive despite long centuries of feudal division quite similar to that of Europe. The Koreans, too, in the seventh century drew together into a politically, culturally, and linguistically unified country, which was thereafter to suffer only very brief intervals of disruption.

Other essentially proto-national groupings, such as those of the Thai and Burmans, probably formed before modern times; but for much of the world the nation state was a relatively recent and sudden development, based almost entirely on the patterns already evolved in Western Europe. Even in Germany and Italy, the nation state was only the product of the second half of the nineteenth century. The pattern spread to Latin America earlier in that century, but it came to much of Asia and most of Africa only in the twentieth. In fact, in many places nation states are still in the process of forming, and their success as permanently viable political units is by no means assured.

The story of the rise of the nation state is complex, but the important point is that, as in the case of the development of earlier units of human cooperation, its growth and consolidation was a long slow process, spread out over many generations. It was not until the past two centuries that the nation state came to be the overwhelmingly important unit of human organization even in Western

Europe. Once the pattern had been fully developed, it spread more rapidly to new areas. But even so, it is taking generations for people to shift their thinking and patterns of conduct from some previous concept of the basic unit of human integration to the nation state.

But now quite suddenly we are being forced to move on to form a much larger and more complex community —the whole world. And we are given, not many generations, but at most a few decades to achieve this. Is mankind capable of this sort of huge psychological change in so short a time? Common sense would suggest not, and the answer would seem to be a certain "No" unless we become aware of the problem and strive mightily to cope with it.

Unfortunately, the alternative to success in forming the new, larger community is far more frightening than it was in earlier periods of transition from smaller, simpler units of organization to larger and more complex ones. In those earlier stages, the alternative was simply to fall back to the previous unit of organization. The failure of the classic empires was no doubt extremely painful for the generations who lived through it, but humanity and civilization on the whole survived in smaller empires or in the confused diversity of feudalism. Prior to the development during the past century of huge concentrations of urban, industrial population, even the failure of the nation state might not have been completely catastrophic. But today, if we fail to develop a viable world community, the collapse of civilization may be total. Mutually exclusive and antagonistic nation states will not provide mankind with a workable pattern for survival in the twenty-first century.

Many people have foreseen the need to develop a world community, but the difficulties that stand in the way are immense. No real community can come into being and survive without a strong sense of shared interests and common identity among its members and the development of considerable skill in the management of its affairs. Unfortunately, we are lacking in both for a world community. There are plenty of pious professions about the unity of the world, but this is not enough. What is needed are strong feelings about a world community on the part of many people—perhaps we should say most people—and great skills in cooperation. These we obviously do not have.

The larger and more complex the unit of basic organization, the greater are the skills needed to operate it and the more clearly understood must be the bonds of shared interests that hold it together. The primitive hunting band needed nothing more than an undefined family-type system of organization and a probably unarticulated but very obvious sense of shared interests. Tribes and agricultural communities required something more, and city states and the early empires a still more complex division of functions, a more sophisticated organization of intragroup relations, and a more explicit formulation of the sense of community. The nation states represent an even more complex stage of development, embracing as they often do a considerable diversity of major subunits. In a small country like Denmark the realization of shared interests is strong and the frictions caused by internal divisions are minimal. The same is true even in a large but highly homogeneous nation like Japan. The United States, however, offers a much more complex case, with its multiple divisions by region, state, county, and municipality, by race, by ethnic and religious groups, and by education, profession, and economic status.

The problems of a sense of common identity and the frictions between subgroupings in even a large and heterogeneous nation like ours pale into insignificance when compared with those of a world community. To all the other divisions is added the great one of national identity —the central focus of the nation state. And the cement of a common culture and easy communication through a common language is lacking. To develop the attitudes and institutions needed to make a world community really viable will be a herculean task.

Great efforts have been made to improve our skills in international cooperation, but the results remain pitifully inadequate. Despite determined attempts over a long period of time to develop international law, it remains little more than a theory without much substance. Many grand schemes for a world order have been dreamed up, but none has shown any real practicability. They have all lacked the essential precondition of a true sense of community.

Take, for example, the old Marxist concept that a fully socialistic world, by eliminating class cleavages—the one cause for human friction to which classical Marxism paid much attention—would produce a unified world of harmonious cooperation between nations. This theory seems no more valid than the Marxist belief that in a socialist state the organs of government would wither away, since presumably the achievement of economic equality through socialism would remove the only real source of conflict or disagreement within countries as well as between them. Socialist states show no tendency to relax their controls over their people or their animosities toward one another, even when an ostensibly classless society has been achieved. In fact, they appear to have expanded their superstructures of government and their controls over their people even more rapidly than have states that are not avowedly following a socialist model. Similarly, in the international field, the relations between so-called socialist states have been far from harmonious, as can be seen from the bitter Sino-Soviet hostility and the repeated military intervention of the Soviet Union in the states of East Europe. Nationalistic tensions seem to be every bit as severe and perhaps even worse among the Communist states than among the so-called capitalist ones or between nations in the two groups.

At the height of the "cold war," some may have felt that a decisive triumph for the so-called free world would produce a peaceful world community capable of facing emerging global problems, but this concept seems no more realistic. A worldwide Pax Americana or even a more broadly based coalition of the "free world" could not have created a true world community willing and able to cooperate on the type of global problems that the world is beginning to face. As we have seen, the less developed two-thirds of the world cannot be coerced into cooperation. A true world community can only be a voluntary association of nations that realize their interdependence and common interests. It cannot be produced by force, and the effort to do so would probably destroy civilization before even this inadequate form of unification had been achieved.

The United Nations is obviously the most ambitious effort to date to develop the spirit and the organs of cooperation for a world community, but it too falls far short of the goal. On the whole, its record is more discouraging than hopeful. Of course, it does represent a definite advance over the League of Nations. Even though the losers in World War II were initially excluded, it has not proved to be as blatant a club of the victors banded together to preserve their gains. It still does not include Germany, Korea, or Vietnam, three of the world's bigger countries that were divided after World War II through external intervention, but at least it does not exclude a large part of the world's population locked away in other peoples' empires, as was the case in the League of Nations. It has built up around it even more organs for effective international cooperation in a number of technical and cultural fields than clustered around the League. As we have seen, it has already lived much longer, being still decidedly alive after more than a quarter century, whereas the League at a younger age had already become the mere ghost of an ephemeral dream.

The United Nations, however, has most certainly not developed into a successful mechanism for solving the really difficult problems of international relations, and the hope that it might in time do so has been steadily fading.

Its very structure precludes the possibility. In the General Assembly the fiction is maintained that all national units are equal. It is much as if the United States or any other large democracy tried to operate on the principle that all municipalities, from the hundred-person village to the multi-million metropolis, had an equal vote on all decisions. In the General Assembly, nations representing less than 5 per cent of the world's population and even less of its wealth and power could form a decisive majority. Obviously, the larger countries are not going to accept decisions by this sort of majority, and thus the General Assembly is not permitted to make any really important decisions.

The Security Council is almost equally ineffectual as a decision-making body. In it, permanent seats and individual veto powers are assigned to five countries which are not the five most populous or strongest units in the world but, shades of the League of Nations, actually represent the five major victors of World War II—the United States, the Soviet Union, the United Kingdom, France, and China. Unfortunately, these five also happen to be the five states with nuclear power, thus creating the strong, even if erroneous, impression that the possession of nuclear weapons is to be equated with having the right to a permanent seat and a veto in the Security Council. The third and fourth richest nations, Japan and West Germany, are missing from the list, obviously because they were among the losers in World War II. India, the second most populous nation, and Indonesia, the fifth, are also missing, because they were still colonies when the United Nations was formed. But whatever may have been the historic or other reasons for giving the veto power to the five nations that have it, there can be little doubt that the Security Council cannot reach decisions on matters in which these nations have seriously divergent views. This is tantamount to saying that it cannot make decisions on any really controversial international problem.

The United Nations, moreover, has no capacity to enforce such decisions as it does make on major nations and very little ability to force them even on small ones. The boldest decision it ever took—to stop the invasion of South Korea by North Korea in 1950—was the result of a fluke, that is, the sulking absence of the Soviet Union from the Security Council, and was in fact largely a sham, because the resulting military action was almost entirely an effort by the United States under a thin legal mantle cast over it by the United Nations. Since the Korean War, the efforts of the United Nations have become steadily less bold and less effective.

The chief political function of the United Nations today seems to be to offer a forum for the expression of world opinion—a sort of Gallup Poll of the nations. In some cases, this may inhibit national actions that go against majority views, though the record is not very convincing on this score. It also offers an opportunity to weaker countries to express their spleen against stronger ones. This may have some therapeutic value. Resentments of past exploitations and fears of future domination are great. Frustrations run deep. It may be psychologically valuable to have a place where such feelings can be aired. But all this makes little positive contribution to solving the real problems the world faces. If anything, it exacerbates frictions and animosities, rather than creating a sense of community through common decisions. In short, the United Nations as it now operates produces the bitterness we know in the domestic political process but not the necessary political decisions. And what movement there is appears to be in the wrong direction. The decision, for example, to ignore Taiwan in the compilation of world statistics, even though this island constitutes a larger economic and political unit than do two-thirds of the countries represented in the United Nations, is clearly a step away from reality and toward sheer partisan politics.

I do not mean to suggest that the United Nations is useless. It remains a symbol of the hope that man can some day achieve a stable world order. Around it also have grown up a large number of institutions for worldwide cooperation in the less controversial areas of human activity, and these probably do contribute to the creation of a sense of world community. One might view the General Assembly and the Security Council as the hole at the center of a doughnut of emerging international institutions. When these surrounding institutions become strong enough and an adequate sense of community has developed, then it may be possible to fill in this hole with a central organ for decision-making on the really difficult world problems.

The inability of the United Nations today to serve as the central political organ of a world community is hardly surprising. No major state would accept it in this role. Communication between the various national groupings of people is far from adequate. The sense of community is still very weak. There is little realization of how interdependent the whole world actually is and how much more so it soon will be. If the United Nations ever becomes an effectively operating political body, this will be possible only because of the prior development of a sense of community in the world. It was never realistic to hope that the reverse would happen—that is, that the existence of an ineffectual United Nations would create a sense of world community.

The development of a new and more complex unit of human organization and cooperation, as we have seen, is a slow and uncertain process. We should, therefore, not be surprised at the failure of the United Nations to live up to the hopes that some people had for it. The creation of a world community cannot be a simple, one-step achievement, any more than the development of the nation state was. The full-fledged nation state did not suddenly march forth from the Middle Ages. Its various elements appeared one by one over a long period of time and only gradually drew together as the unified nation state we have known in recent times.

Similarly, the creation of a world community will be a multi-faceted and complex process, spanning a wide variety of human activities and requiring a great number of interrelated steps. In certain fields, the process is moving ahead rapidly. This is true of international cooperation in the more technical and less controversial fields. It is also the case in much of the world in economic relations, such as trade and the operations of multi-national corporations, and in cultural and popular activities, from music and literary translations, through sports and tourism, to the dissemination of news. But in the crucial field of mechanisms for making the fundamental international political and economic decisions on which man's fate may well depend, it is as yet moving only very slowly.

This situation is probably inevitable. Effective cooperation in political matters can only follow, rather than precede, a realization of its necessity. This in turn depends on the development of pervasive interrelationships, shared interests, and a clear recognition of the fact that the ultimate fate of men everywhere is deeply intertwined. The national units into which the world is presently divided can form a unified body for effective decision making on the truly difficult problems mankind faces only if these nations and their peoples really feel united.

Seen in the light of history, the complexity of the problem and the slowness of our progress seem reasons for despair. How can men possibly achieve what is needed in the brief time that seems available? We should not be too discouraged, however. Progress is being made toward the creation of a world community. This is to be seen not so much in the pathetically inadequate attempt to achieve it in one jump through the United Nations, as in a series of less all-inclusive beginnings at building international groupings. These are probably the necessary way stations on the road to the development of a global community, and it is to them that we should next address our attention.

5 ♗ REGIONAL AND TRANS-REGIONAL GROUPINGS

A fourteenth-century European would have found it difficult to foretell the course by which the modern nation state would evolve, even if he had had some concept of the end product. We today, living in a vastly more complex world, cannot do much better in predicting the route by which a world community may be achieved and the problems which will be encountered on the way, even though the desired result is clearer in our minds and the time in which it must be accomplished is to be measured in decades rather than centuries. We can, however, look around us at some of the international groupings that already do exist and at the problems they face for the light these may throw on the still larger problems of the formation of a world community.

Regional groupings of nations are undoubtedly helping to provide the building blocks out of which a world community can be constructed. They are also contributing to the development of the necessary skills in international relations. The outstanding example is the European Economic Community, originally consisting of France, West Germany, Italy, and the three small Benelux countries—The Netherlands, Belgium, and Luxembourg. This grouping has recently become even more important by the inclusion of the United Kingdom, Denmark, and Ireland.

When one remembers the long history of enmity and war between the English, French, Germans, and Italians, the European Community is an astounding achievement. Progress has been uneven—by starts and stops—but it has been significant. Even a powerful figure like De Gaulle, who seemed on such matters a spiritual throwback to the eighteenth century, could not block the forward movement permanently. The concept of community has grown steadily and is succinctly expressed in the name itself. The necessity of subsuming national interests in community interests is gradually becoming clearer. The European Community represents a far greater advance over the interstate relations of Western Europe in the interwar years than the United Nations does over the League of Nations.

Most other regional groupings, as in Latin America, Africa, the Middle East, and Southeast Asia, seem by comparison weak and immature. The difference may be essentially that between advanced, industrialized nations, which have extensive relationships with one another and closely shared interests, and less developed countries, which have much thinner contacts. The members of the European Community are all relatively affluent, industrialized nations with comparable standards of living and similar political and social institutions. A large part of their foreign trade and cultural and intellectual contacts are with one another.

The countries in the other regional groupings may have similar cultural backgrounds, comparable social and political institutions, and a common low standard of living but, in contrast to the Western European states, they usually have little natural trade with one another and often only weak cultural and intellectual links. Since they are largely preindustrial, tropical or subtropical countries, their exports are largely minerals and tropical agricultural products, which are likely to be similar to those of the other countries in the region. Their natural trading partners are therefore not their neighbors but more distant industrialized countries, which have the largest markets for these products and produce the manufactured goods these less industrialized countries cannot yet produce for themselves. The moral of the success of the European Community and the weakness of the other regional groupings should be clear: shared interests precede effective cooperation.

The so-called Atlantic community might be considered by some to be a super-regional grouping, embracing as it does the great North American nations of the United States and Canada, together with the countries of the European Community. The total area is broad, straddling the North Atlantic and helping to illustrate the fact that in this age of cheap and easy maritime transportation even large bodies of water serve more to bring distant areas together economically than to divide them. As in the case of the European Community, the members of the still larger and looser Atlantic community have roughly comparable standards of living, a common cultural background, similar social and political institutions, huge economic relations with one another, and a great variety of other contacts. Out of all this has emerged a realization of shared interests and interdependence and a growing sense of community.

Thus we see that, at least in industrially advanced areas, regional groupings are beginning to add a higher level of effective integration above that of the nation state. In this sense, regional units may constitute a useful step toward a world community, but it seems doubtful that they themselves will amalgamate together into such a community through any quick and simple process of federation. My reason for this skepticism is that, in transcending the old narrow national limits of human cooperation, regional groupings usually emphasize other exclusive even if broader limitations, such as shared historical backgrounds, common cultural traits, and similar racial composition.

Among the less developed nations, regional solidarity has often been frankly expressed in terms of hostility to other groups—Latin Americans against Yanqui and European exploiters, Africans against white ex-colonialists, Arabs against Israel and the West, Southeast Asians against the dangers of Chinese, Japanese, or American domination. Even in the case of the European and Atlantic communities, hostility and exclusiveness toward others have figured in their formation. A desire to balance the overwhelming economic power of the United States was one of the reasons for the creation of the European Economic Community, and both it and the Atlantic community also grew in large part out of NATO (the North Atlantic Treaty Organization) and the American effort to restore the war-torn economies of Western Europe, both of which were undertakings designed to counter the threat of Soviet domination over Western Europe. To the peoples of the less developed countries, moreover, the European and Atlantic communities appear as groupings designed to perpetuate Western economic and possibly political dominance over the rest of the world. In other words, they look like exclusive clubs of the richer and more successful members of Western civilization and the white race, whose rule over most of the world in recent centuries is still deeply resented and whose continuing economic domination is greatly feared.

Regional groupings thus, while helping to transcend some national rivalries and frictions, run the danger of emphasizing interregional hostilities and suspicions, which often are strengthened by cultural and racial tensions. The once great geographic distances between the major races and cultures of the world and the intensity of rivalries among nations within the same region, culture, and race have in the past somewhat obscured the depth of distrust and hostility between differing cultures and races, but divisions of this sort are probably much greater fault lines in humanity than are national distinctions. They may be all the more serious in our age because the line between the bulk of Western civilization and the white race on the one side and the other major civilizations and races on the other is underlain for the most part by another dangerous fault line—that between the industrialized, prosperous countries and the preindustrial, poor ones. Among the nonwhite, non-Western nations, only Japan lies clearly on the affluent side of this line; among the white countries of Western civilization, only some of those in Latin America and possibly parts of Southern Europe lie on the poorer side.

A world in which regional communities of relatively homogeneous culture and race grow constantly stronger but are held together only by an ineffective worldwide organization like the United Nations is a frightening prospect. In place of the rivalries and tensions between nations, which have kept mankind in intermittent warfare over the centuries, we might find ourselves facing even more dangerous intercultural and interracial conflicts.

Regionalism itself thus is no international panacea. It can be helpful in producing peace and prosperity within the regions concerned. It can foster the development of skills in international relations. It can be a useful sub-integration in the broader world community. The three Benelux countries have shown by their union, their participation in the larger European Community, and their membership in the still larger Atlantic community that countries can belong to a whole series of communities existing at different levels. Regional groupings therefore do not have to stand in the way of a culminating integration into a world community. But the further strengthening of regional communities will not of itself automatically lead to the development of the necessary world community and could actually work against it.

There fortunately does exist a more promising start toward a world community than any of the regional communities, with their geographic, cultural, and racial exclusiveness, could be. This is the trans-regional groupings of interdependent, industrialized nations I have referred to in earlier chapters, which centers on the great triangle of Western Europe, North America, and Japan but also includes some other industrialized nations, such as Australia. Since it lacks any accepted name—sometimes it is rather vaguely and incongruously called the "West"—we might for convenience refer to it as "the triangular community." It can be defined as the major industrialized, trading nations of the world, the one modifier excluding the still largely preindustrial, less developed countries and the other modifier the industrialized Communist states, which as a matter of national policy emphasize economic autarky and a controlled society and therefore keep their foreign trade and other contacts strictly limited.

Some may think of this triangular community as merely a minor extension of the Atlantic community, necessitated by Japan's rapid rise as an economic power and symbolized by its admission in 1964 into the O.E.C.D. (the Organization for Economic Cooperation and Development), which is sometimes referred to as the club of the rich, industrialized nations. As seen at the time, the inclusion of Japan was indeed only a small expansion of the Atlantic community, somewhat reluctantly accepted by its European members; but in a broader historical perspective it was an extremely significant step. Not only has Japan become the second most productive national unit in the triangular community, but its membership takes this community a much longer step toward the achievement of a world community than the Atlantic community by itself could ever have done.

For one thing, the triangular community has less of the negative overtones of the Atlantic community. The latter, as we have seen, came into being in large part as a reaction against the supposed threat of the Soviet Union. The triangular community, while not lacking in a defense component—as is symbolized by the continuation of NATO and the Mutual Security Treaty between Japan and the United States—is focused much more on global economic relationships. It is a spontaneous grouping together of nations with close economic and intellectual ties and with deeply shared interests. In other words, it is not just a defense alliance held together by negative external forces but a voluntary association of nations over a wide area joined together by positive mutual interests.

An even more important point is that the triangular grouping is trans-cultural and trans-racial. As we have seen, the Altantic community can all too easily appear to others as a banding together of most of the major white nations that were in recent centuries the imperialist rulers of the world. (Only Russia is left out but has its own exclusive East European club.) As such, it may seem to be the antithesis of an acceptable pattern for a world community.

The triangular community, on the other hand, even though it still may be a club of the rich, industrialized nations, shows through Japan's membership that it is not limited solely to countries of Western civilization and the white race. The economic rise of Japan in recent times and its ability to win its way into this grouping of great industrialized nations give promise that other countries, regardless of their race or culture, can cross the line of industrialization and affluence to become full members of the club. In fact, it suggests that in time the bulk of the world and eventually all of it can become members of a single community of deeply shared interests and interdependence. For this reason, the triangular grouping may well represent the beginning of a world community or at least an early prototype for one.

We should not, however, overemphasize the solidarity of the triangular community. It is a much less close and sharply defined grouping than the European Community. It has no clear structure or discrete organs of government. It has no authority over its members except insofar as they voluntarily accept the decisions of the group as a whole. It is nonetheless a real community of nations in a way the United Nations is not.

The United Nations, as the product of conscious design, has a clear structure and multiple organs with well-defined functions and authority, but it lacks the life-blood of shared interests and a sense of community. The triangular community in contrast is the natural product of massive relations, close interdependence, and a growing sense of shared interest. These relations and shared interests are in large part economic, but they also embrace other fields—cultural, intellectual, scientific, and strategic. There can be no doubt that industrialized nations such as these find one another overwhelmingly their best markets, as well as the best sources for a large part of their imports. They also exchange technology, and their great business firms have become complexly intertwined. Their scientists and scholars cooperate intimately with one another, and there is a vast flow of cultural influences and of people between them.

The overlapping interests among these nations and their similar views of world problems make them natural military allies. In fact, war between them has now become quite unthinkable. The historian perhaps will bridle at this phrase, remembering its premature use before World War I and during the euphoria that followed its end. But the relationships among these countries are vastly greater and their interdependence and shared interest much more strongly felt now than at these earlier times. Whereas warfare between many of the members of the United Nations is all too possible, a war between any of the members of the triangular community could come about only after a long and catastrophic decline in their relations, not suddenly as in the recent past.

The organs of cooperation within the triangular community have followed the development of shared interests and the growth of a sense of community, not preceded them. As a consequence, the formal bodies for consultation and decision making within the community are not neatly logical but remain somewhat haphazard—as is true of most really living human institutions. The community does not even have an accepted name, except for a series of acronyms, each of which refers to an organization that is concerned with certain aspects of the economic activities of the community. There are, for example, the O.E.C.D., the GATT (General Agreement on Tariffs and Trade), and the IMF (International Monetary Fund). While these and various similar organizations often include other countries, they are all dominated by the nations of the triangular community. But perhaps more important than any of these formal organizations for the coordination of the community's activities are the endless series of meetings held among its political leaders, from Presidents and Prime Ministers on down, and also among its businessmen, scientists, scholars, and simple citizens.

(handwritten annotations on diagram: "triangular community", "pre industrial society", "communists")

For all its amorphousness, the triangular community probably represents the greatest advance toward the development of a global community and therefore toward world peace made in the generation since World War II. Its importance cannot be overemphasized. It is clearly a closer approach than are other existing international groupings to what a true world community might be. But we should examine a little more closely the concept that it might indeed grow into a world community or at least show the way in which one could be developed.

The triangular community can be viewed as occupying only one angle of a still larger triangle that embraces the whole human race. The other two angles would then consist of the industrialized Communist nations and the still largely preindustrial, less developed countries. The population of the triangular community amounts to only about a fifth of that of the whole larger triangle, but in wealth it comes close to possessing two-thirds of the total. Its huge economic strength exerts a tremendous gravitational pull on the industrialized Communist nations, and it is possible that, as they develop more international trade and open themselves to more contacts with the outside world, they will in time be drawn at least into a tandem relationship with the existing triangular community. There are many signs that this may in fact be beginning to happen. The differences in internal organization and in external points of view between the Communist and non-Communist industrialized nations are so great that any very close community embracing them both is not easy to imagine, but hostility and frictions seem to be declining between them and long-range, shared interests appear to be on the rise.

While the relationship between the two groups of industrialized nations has loomed largest in the minds of people in both groups, it is probable that a far greater problem lies in their relationship with the third angle of the triangle of humanity—that is, with the less developed nations, which have more than two-thirds of the world's population but only one-sixth of its present productive power. Indeed, a strengthening of the bonds between the Communist and non-Communist industrialized nations could produce an even sharper line of cleavage between the then more unified rich countries and the poorer ones, or even a blatant effort by the former to control the latter.

The basic question concerning the less developed countries of the world is whether a start can be made soon enough in closing the tragic gap in wealth and opportunity between them and the industrialized countries before global problems have grown beyond control and advancing technology has brought the world together into a critically explosive mass. If the gap can be closed enough to permit the presently less developed countries to have a self-respecting, meaningful role in world affairs and they can thus develop massive relations and truly shared interests with the industrialized nations, then they too will in time become full members of a world community. In fact, some of them already are beginning to achieve this status. I have in mind some of the more successful states of Latin America and even of Asia and possibly Africa. Others undoubtedly will follow if they can only develop their economies and institutions rapidly enough and there proves to be sufficient time for this to happen.

The present triangular community, which, though an economic majority, is in population only a relatively small minority, does therefore have the possibility of expanding to become a great majority in population also and eventually to embrace the whole world. I would not predict that this is the course the world will follow, but it or something analogous to it seems to me to be the most likely way a true world community might ultimately come into being.

On the other hand, if the triangular community were to atrophy or disintegrate, as it sometimes shows signs of doing, into three regional blocs—a North American, a Western European, and a Japanese—or even into two blocs—an Atlantic and a Japanese—this would be a long step away from the creation of the needed world community. The pull on the industrialized Communist countries to join the community or develop a closer relationship with it would weaken. The industrialized trading nations would be even less able than now to develop common policies for conserving natural resources and controlling global pollution. Racial and cultural tensions would certainly increase between the nonwhite, non-Western Japanese bloc and the others. There would be little hope that the various blocs could work together effectively on the problem of closing the gap between themselves and the less developed nations. Each bloc would probably develop its own backyard of semi-dependent, less developed countries, and tensions between each of them and its economic backyard would undoubtedly mount, as the less developed nations perceived the more exclusive relationship with only one of the industrialized areas as neo-colonial domination. For example, Southeast Asia, even under present conditions, is showing signs of developing the attitudes of profound distrust and hostility toward Japan that have for so long characterized the relationship between Latin America and the United States. A deterioration of the triangular community would lessen in a number of ways the possibility that the human race can cope with the global problems that lie ahead.

6 ⊕ THE PROBLEMS OF
A WORLD COMMUNITY

Whether or not the present triangular community of the industrialized trading nations proves to be the embryo of a future, more unitary world, its experience and difficulties may help us visualize what sorts of problems a world community will face. Other aspects of international relations—such as the global balance of power, the tensions between the industrialized and nonindustrialized parts of the world, and the multitudinous frictions among the less developed countries—will all no doubt continue into the future as important though already familiar international problems. But the strains within the triangular community perhaps best illustrate the newer types of problems that a developing world community will encounter, and they therefore deserve careful analysis.

Growth and rapid change have proved as upsetting to the triangular community as they usually have to other human institutions. Recently, they have produced signs of tension and discord that are all the more alarming because of the possible role of this informal grouping of major countries as a harbinger of a true world community.

Three factors of growth and change account at least in part for the present difficulties. One has been the expansion of the European Community (one of the major components of the larger grouping) to include the United Kingdom and other smaller countries and the tightening of the bonds within this subgroup as a whole. The result has been the need for some readjustments in the relationship between this smaller, more closely knit, regional community and the other members of the larger, less unified triangular community.

The second factor is the change that has been going on in the United States for the past few years. A period of urgent economic and social adjustment between the various subgroupings within the country has coincided with a period of adjustment of the American role in the world. Emerging from World War II as by far the richest and strongest nation and the only major power not seriously hurt by the conflict, the United States played for long a preponderant world role. It became widely enmeshed in local problems as the "world's policeman" and, we might add, "economic angel," developing in the process attitudes of self-righteous arrogance. With the economic recovery of the devastated industrialized nations and the rapid political rise of the less developed countries, the relative American position in the world declined more rapidly than its actual role. The adjustment to this situation was complicated by domestic changes taking place at the same time, and both adjustments were made much more painful and acute than they otherwise might have been by anguish over the failure of American policy in Vietnam and the strong feeling of many Americans that military involvement in Southeast Asia had been morally wrong. Americans have been confused, political feelings have run high, and debate has been acrimonious.

There has been serious anxiety over specific issues, such as the future of the economy, the balance of payments, and American commitments and responsibilities abroad, as well as a deeper questioning of the basic values of American society. Under these circumstances, the United States, once the stable anchor member of the triangular community, has become a somewhat unpredictable touchy participant.

The third and undoubtedly most upsetting change has been the explosive rise of Japan as an industrial giant. For more than a decade its GNP (gross national product) has grown at an average of more than 10 per cent per year in real terms—that is, after having subtracted monetary gains due to inflation. As a result, Japan has been doubling in economic size every seven years, and its foreign trade has been expanding even faster. At this rate, its GNP multiplies eightfold in two decades and its foreign trade sixteen times. Since it has been growing at more than twice the speed of the United States and most other countries, its relative position in the world's economy has risen sharply, upsetting previous balances between it and the rest of the world, especially the United States, with which it has for years done about 30 per cent of its total trade.

For Americans the rather sudden shift from surpluses in their balance of trade with Japan to a deficit measured in the billions of dollars has been a particularly shocking aspect of the present time of trouble. Some adjustment of this situation has seemed to them imperative. But the shift among the Japanese in their concept of Japan's position in the world has been perhaps an even more upsetting product of Japan's rapid economic growth. Ever since World War II, Japanese have assumed that their country had to subordinate its foreign policy to that of the United States. This attitude was understandable in view of their defeat by the United States in that war, the seven years of American military occupation that followed it, the continuing years of dependence on the United States by a still economically weak Japan, and then a longer period in which the Japanese leaders chose to maintain a "low posture" in foreign affairs, safely in the lea of American policy, in order to free themselves to concentrate on Japan's economic growth. This position of assumed subordination to the United States, however, is no longer tolerable to a people who are now very much aware that they are economically the third most powerful country in the world and in many ways the most smoothly operating major industrial nation. To them, an adjustment in political relations with the United States seems even more important than an adjustment in the economic field.

If Japan is not to be dependent on the United States in foreign policy, then the alternative in Japanese minds is for it to be independent—or "autonomous," as they usually phrase the concept. But what does independence or autonomy mean? Do they imply rivalry and eventual hostility? As we have seen, Japan and the United States have massive relations with each other of all sorts, and for the most part their interests are complementary rather than conflicting. For example, they have developed between each other the largest transoceanic trade the world has ever known. Under these circumstances, and in a world in which international relations are growing at an accelerating speed, the natural alternatives to subordination and dependence would seem to be equality and interdependence. These should be taken for granted if there really is a triangular community that includes Japan. Why are they not automatically accepted in Japan as the obvious goals? The answer to this question, I believe, throws a great deal of light on what the chief problems are in the existing triangular community and what they are likely to be in a future world community.

The elements of greatest promise in the triangular community, which are its worldwide extent and its straddling of cultural and racial lines, also appear to be its chief weaknesses. There are far greater strains between Japan on the one side and North America and Western Europe on the other than between the latter two, which are close in culture and race. Profound and deeply felt cleavages between major cultures and races existed, of course, in previous times, but in this age of growing regional cooperation on the one hand and shrunken geographic distance between major racial and cultural groupings on the other, they show signs of becoming much more difficult and crucial problems than they ever were before. They may well turn out to be the unbridgeable chasms on the road to a world community. The tensions between Japan and the other members of the triangular community loom, not just as a difficult problem at this particular time in this special grouping of nations, but as a possibly crucial test case for the future of the whole world.

The growing interdependence of the world is, of course, no clearer to Japanese than to others, nor are they any more aware of the natural forces that have produced the close bonds and common interests of the triangular community. Japanese thinking, like ours, is much more conditioned by balance of power concepts. To them, the most obvious aspect of the relationship with the United States is the Mutual Security Treaty, whereby the United States maintains military bases in Japan and is committed to its defense from external aggression. This emphasis in Japan on the military aspect of the relationship is natural, because the defense treaty evolved from the postwar American military occupation of Japan, which had a pervasive impact on the nation, and American military bases and personnel in Japan remain as constantly irritating reminders of this past phase of American military domination. In the eyes of many Japanese, the Security Treaty continues to relegate Japan to a position of military and political subordination to the United States—or worse, to a role as catspaw of American imperialism. Furthermore, because of differences in language, culture, and race, American bases in Japan are inevitably a far greater political irritant than they are in European countries, where the barriers to understanding between foreign soldiers and the local population loom less high.

The Japanese thus have tended to see the relationship with the United States largely in military terms. Specifically, they have considered the Security Treaty as placing them in a perilous front-line position in the bipolar or triangular balance between the United States and the Soviet Union and China. To some, this seemed the inevitable result of geography, and a secure place on the American side of the seesaw appeared far better than a position on the other side. To others, the fact that they were on the balance of power seesaw at all seemed merely the product of the treaty. They saw it, not as giving Japan security, but as imperiling Japan by involving it in a dangerously aggressive American policy in East Asia. To such persons the wisest course appeared to be to get safely off the seesaw by renouncing the treaty and maintaining a position of careful neutrality, equidistant between China, the Soviet Union, and the United States. The expansion of the Vietnam War after 1965 greatly increased such feelings, and wide revulsion against American actions in Vietnam made the whole problem of a shared defense with the United States an extremely touchy issue.

The controversy over the Security Treaty is an old story in Japan, but the development in the past few years of the concept of a five-power balance of power has injected a new element into it which is highly disturbing for both sides in the debate. It seems to suggest that Japan must not only make haste to balance its relations with the United States by establishing equally close relations with China and the Soviet Union, but also that it should greatly increase its own military power in order to hold down one of the five corners in the new world order. Neither concept is realistic. The autarkic economies and closed societies of China and the Soviet Union make it impossible for Japan to establish as great and close relations with these countries as it has with the United States; and the strong pacifistic yearnings of the Japanese people and the extreme sensitivity of all their neighbors to Japanese military power make any rapid rearmament extremely distasteful to all concerned and, in my judgment, profoundly unwise.

The main point I am trying to make here, however, is

that balance of power concepts have greatly impeded the perception in Japan of the emerging triangular community and its vast importance for Japan and the world. As I see the situation, the Security Treaty is only one aspect of Japan's relations with only one other member in that community. Since there is no very credible military threat to Japan, with or without American bases there, the main value of this treaty may be merely to give the Japanese a sense of security, so that they do not feel impelled to embark on rapid rearmament. The presence of the American Seventh Fleet in the Western Pacific and the American commitment to the defense of South Korea, both of which would probably be impossible without the treaty, may contribute to that sense of security. In any case, I believe that it is up to the Japanese to decide what security arrangements they wish with the United States, and for the United States then to see to what extent it can comply with Japanese desires. But whatever happens to the Security Treaty, a close Japanese-American relationship as a major aspect of the triangular community is of vital importance to both countries and to the world.

Most Japanese would probably agree that Japan's relationship with the United States and the other members of the triangular community is of supreme importance to it, but they have serious doubts about the reliability of the United States, to say nothing of the European powers, as partners for Japan. For example, even among those who value the American defense relationship, there has been a growing suspicion that Americans are far more likely to live up to commitments to countries of similar race and culture, such as Australia, the United Kingdom, or Germany, than to Japan. They wonder if the United States would risk the fate of New York in order to defend Tokyo, as it might to protect London. They ask themselves if Americans can truly feel a sense of common interest with nations that are not Caucasian in race and Western in culture. This point of view is obviously "racist," to use the term so commonly employed in domestic debate, but "racism" is probably as grave an international issue as it has ever been a domestic American problem. It runs deep in all the Asian countries I know well and, as far as I can judge, is strong in most parts of the world.

The Japanese anxiety that American defense commitments to them are not very reliable merges with the fear that all Westerners may be incapable of treating a non-Western, nonwhite people like the Japanese as full equals. These are really the twin aspects of a single issue that constitutes the nub of the whole problem, at least from the Japanese point of view.

There is a long history behind such attitudes. For several centuries, the great nations of Western culture and white race dominated most of the world. In 1854, Japan was forced against its will to open relations with the West on the latter's terms. For several generations, the Japanese scrambled desperately to ensure their political and economic security by matching Western military and industrial power. They also meekly sought to win Western respect by conforming to Western norms. The memory of those days was recently freshened by the American military occupation of a defeated Japan and political tutelage over it. Japanese remain sensitive about their inescapable subservience to the West in the past and dubious that Occidentals have greatly changed, or perhaps can ever really change, their traditional attitudes of racial and cultural superiority.

There is no denying that racial and cultural prejudices have colored American relations with Japan and East Asia in the past. The blatant discrimination against Japanese and other Orientals on the West Coast in the early decades of this century and the complete exclusion of Japanese in 1924 on purely racial grounds needlessly worsened American relations with Japan. The only reason such acts did not also threaten American relations with other Asian lands was that none of the others had governments that could put up much of a protest.

Of course, the Japanese have not been free of racial and cultural biases either. These showed up in their assumption in the years leading up to World War II that Americans were such personally selfish and effete people that they lacked the will power to fight a long war to redress any swift and bold move by Japan. When such attitudes were met by comparable cultural and racial contempt on the part of Americans, war perhaps became inevitable.

Cultural and racial prejudice can clearly be seen in Washington's refusal to take either Japanese diplomatic arguments or military threats very seriously in those crucial prewar years. Americans could not really bring themselves to believe that these "little yellow men" would dare to challenge the United States, and the American military for the most part was quite sure that the Japanese would prove no great threat if they did. It was widely said that all Japanese had bad eyes and therefore could not fly planes properly and that in any case they were merely a nation of inept imitators. The brilliant Japanese success at Pearl Harbor was all the more traumatic to Americans because of such attitudes of racial prejudice and therefore helped trigger hysterical reactions, such as the completely unjustified rounding up into concentration camps of all persons of Japanese ancestry on the West Coast.

Many Japanese believe that in World War II, Americans were more ready to drop the atom bomb on them, a people of different race, than they would have been on Germans. I feel that they are quite wrong in this idea and that the choice of the target country was merely an accident of the timing of the development of the bomb, but this other interpretation persists. There are similar feelings—I believe with considerably more justification—that the horrors of American bombing in Vietnam and incidents such as the one at My Lai would have been less likely if the opponent had been of Caucasian race and Western culture.

General MacArthur's decision to move ahead in a strategically unsound advance into North Korea in 1950, when there were clear signs of impending Chinese intervention if we persisted, was obviously based on his unwarranted assumption that "Orientals" would respect firmness and power and could be outbluffed. The Chinese called his bluff and administered to better armed American troops the worst single defeat the United States has ever suffered. Once again, in the bombing of North Vietnam, Americans assumed that the will of Asians to resist would crumble under such pressure, even though they had discovered that similar bombings in World War II had only strengthened the British and German resolve to fight on. Thus once again racial bias led to disastrously wrong decisions.

The Nixon Doctrine, first enunciated by the President on Guam in July of 1969, has more recently added to Japanese doubts about the reliability of Americans as partners and their ability to accept non-Westerners as equals. The original purpose of the statement, I believe, was to make clear that the United States would not again become involved in a war like that in Vietnam and that it recognized that the defense of any less developed country depended basically on the will of its own people, while the American contribution could at most be only supplementary. This seems to me an eminently sound general rule. But the emphasis on "Asia" in the later elaborations of the doctrine and on "Asian boys fighting Asian wars" gave a geographic context to the doctrine that appears to have cultural and racial overtones. There is no corresponding statement about "European boys fighting European wars." Is the point that Asians, including Japanese, being of a different race and culture from Americans, should not expect the same degree of defense commitment from the United States as would Europeans or Australians? Certainly many Japanese have read the Nixon Doctrine in this way.

Perhaps the recent incident that has most seriously undermined Japanese trust in the reliability of the United States as a partner and belief in the ability of Americans to treat Japanese as equals was the sudden rapprochement of the United States with China, heralded by the visit of Dr. Kissinger to Peking in July 1971 and consummated in part through President Nixon's visit to China in February 1972. Not that Japanese opposed the rapprochement itself. Some, thinking in old balance of power terms, may feel that a bettering of Sino-American relations automatically means a worsening of Japanese-American relations. Past history gives some justification to such a view, though present conditions, I feel, make it nonsense. The Japanese on the whole, however, welcomed the rapprochement between the United States and China. It was what they had for long been urging, and it seemed to them to lessen tensions in their part of the world. What bothered them was not the rapprochement but the way it was achieved, because this seemed to signal a most disturbing attitude on the part of the United States toward Japan.

Relations with China have always loomed much larger in Japan than they have in the United States. This is because of geographic propinquity, tremendous involvements in China during the past century, a fascination for what is going on there next door to Japan, and deeply felt cultural and racial ties. The Japanese have an often-used phrase for these ties—*dōbun dōshu*, meaning "the same culture, the same race." Until they themselves were able to normalize their relations with Peking in September 1972, they felt very unhappy about the lack of diplomatic relations. This was a major issue at the very heart of Japanese domestic political controversy, in a way it never was in the United States. The lack of close relations with China seemed to most Japanese not only unnatural but very dangerous. They blamed it on the United States, because it was American insistence in 1951 and 1952, before they had won back their independence, that had forced them to recognize the Nationalist government on Taiwan instead of Peking. Of course, in more recent years the Japanese government had stuck to this political posture of its own free choice for fear of damaging economic relations with Taiwan. It also had worked out a very successful policy of "separating economics and politics," permitting Japan to become by far China's largest trading partner, even though it did not recognize Peking. But the Japanese public continued to blame Japan's unsatisfactory relationship with China on American intransigence.

The United States government, for its part, always urged Tokyo to coordinate its China policy with that of Washington, and it repeatedly promised close and full consultation. Such consultations were in fact held constantly, and the Japanese government did hew close to the American policy line. As it became apparent that a time of change in China policy was approaching, the Japanese government reassured its public that Japan and the United States would stay in close step with each other on this difficult problem. But when the United States finally did take a large and dramatic step, it not only failed to consult with Tokyo, but did not even notify it in advance.

Japanese feelings were, of course, hurt, and Prime Minister Sato was humiliated. But this was not the real problem. Millions of Sato's political opponents in Japan may actually have been delighted to see him humiliated, but all Japanese were deeply disturbed by the American action, because they saw it as clear evidence either that the United States was willing to sacrifice its good relations with Japan in the hope of bettering its relations with China or else that Americans paid so little attention to Japan that they were quite unmindful of what Japanese thought. The insult was all the greater for being perhaps quite unconscious. To Japanese it seemed to show how little hope there was that Americans could learn to deal with them as true equals. They doubted that the United States would have treated Europeans so cavalierly.

These doubts that exercise the Japanese in their relations with the United States and also with the other countries of the triangular community do not loom so large in the minds of Americans and Europeans. To them, the economic frictions with Japan constitute the big issue. Major problems have indeed been generated by the meteoric rise of the Japanese economy and the huge flow of exports and huge balance of payments surpluses this has produced. Many industries in the United States and Europe feel threatened, labor unions inveigh against the "export" of jobs to Japan, and the American government and public were thunderstruck by a $4 billion deficit in trade with Japan in the single year of 1972. The Japanese economic challenge has been a major reason for a series of international economic earthquakes, such as President Nixon's new economic policy of August 1971, when the United States placed a 10 per cent surcharge on imports and floated the dollar; the subsequent revaluation of world currencies, in which the Japanese yen rose 16.88 per cent as measured against the dollar; and the second round of revaluation in early 1973 when the yen again rose comparably. Earthquakes of this sort are likely to continue.

Economic problems such as these tend to work themselves out over the long run through currency adjustments and the shifts in the costs of exports these and other changing factors produce; but over the short run, unless they are skillfully handled, they can give rise to serious political as well as economic strains. They could set off a massive turning of the tide away from the relatively free trade policies that helped create the triangular community and back toward widespread protectionism of a sort that could wreck the community and recreate the regional economic blocs that proved so disastrous in the 1930's. The hazard of this happening may be all the greater because the economic discord between Japan and the other members of the triangular community seems to carry with it some dangerous racial and cultural overtones. Japanese doubts about the reliability of the United States and the ability of Americans and Europeans to treat them on a basis of full equality are reciprocated by deep suspicions of Japan on cultural and racial grounds on the part of Americans and Europeans.

While the Russians in their animosities toward the Chinese have revived in rather primitive form the old "yellow peril" myth, Americans and Western Europeans, at least in Japanese eyes, have developed a more subtle economic form of this bias. The countries of Western Europe have all along put severe restrictions on the importation of Japanese goods, and, when Americans became deeply worried about their economy and their balance of payment problems, they seemed to view the flow of imports from Japan as much more threatening than that from Europe. Toyotas on American roads somehow appeared more menacing than Volkswagens ever had. Japanese textiles caused far more political uproar than Italian shoes. And when protectionist sentiment against

Japanese imports rose in the United States, Europeans became almost paranoid about the danger that the flow of Japanese goods might be shunted from American shores to theirs.

The rapid rise of Japan's industry and therefore of its exports is, of course, one reason for the special concern in the United States and Europe over Japanese goods. But there seems to be something more lying behind these anxieties. Both in North America and Europe, Japanese are considered as somehow more menacing economically because they seem alien and hard to understand. Their extraordinary efficiency in organizing relations between government and business and between management and labor, instead of winning admiration and where possible emulation, has earned them the somewhat sinister title of "Japan, Inc." Japanese economic strength is widely attributed, not just to their efficiency and hard work, but to exploitative low wages accepted by a docile, faceless, populace. In reality, a powerful labor movement has already forced Japanese wages up above those of the southern tier of Western European countries and may soon push them above the wage scales of the northern European states. But the stereotype remains of an antlike society of a hundred million hardworking, emotionless little yellow people, apparently set on burying the rest of us economically as deep as Stalin threatened to bury us politically.

Even less prejudiced minds are disturbed at the obtuseness of the Japanese in recognizing the economic problems the United States faces and their often ruthless exploitation of the economic weaknesses of the less developed countries. Here the blame lies basically with the

Japanese. Nursing their anxieties about the outside world and living in relative cultural isolation, they have proved imperceptive to the viewpoints of other countries and slow in responding to foreign needs. They have permitted an image to develop abroad of a Japan intent on taking advantage of the relatively open economies of other countries, while keeping its own safely insulated from foreign penetration, not so much by the traditional barriers of tariffs and quotas, as by entanglements of red tape, a veil of impenetrable language, and clannish collusion against the *gaijin* or "outsider." They have seemed purposely inscrutable, preferring to keep their thoughts to themselves behind their high language barriers, while methodically collecting information on the rest of the world that would be useful to them. And they have seemed even more self-centered and rapacious in their dealings with the less developed countries than have the other industrialized nations.

The term "economic animal" for the Japanese, when first used, was meant to suggest that the Japanese had only their own selfish economic interests at heart and had no concern about the broader problems of the world. A military variant of this charge is that of the "free ride," which some Americans have used to accuse the Japanese of taking advantage of costly American defense of Japan, while selfishly refusing to make any substantial contribution themselves and engaging at the same time in irresponsible criticism of American efforts in Japan's behalf. All in all, a picture has taken shape of a Japan that is too egocentric, too aloof, and above all too alien to be a fully acceptable member of a real community of nations.

All these doubts, suspicions, and misunderstandings

could probably be cleared up or at least mitigated if there were adequate communication between Japan and the other members of the triangular community, but unfortunately this is not the case. While all the others speak languages of the same family, write these with the same letters, and use a common idiom and structure of thought derived from a shared cultural background, the Japanese speak an entirely different type of language, written in a wholly different and extremely difficult writing system, and utilize idioms and a structure of thought drawn from a sharply different cultural background. It is not surprising that they communicate only with great difficulty and serious limitations in any of the Western languages and that the other members of the community can communicate hardly at all in Japanese. The simple language barriers alone are enormous between the Japanese and the rest.

This problem is complicated by other subtler but possibly equally important problems of communication. Take for example the styles of dialogue or bargaining Japanese and Americans normally employ. Americans tend to have an assertive manner that borders on overstatement. Japanese, accustomed to a tight, homogeneous society, rely on a more indirect, ambiguous style, designed to avoid confrontations and find compromises. The result is that what Americans have to say resounds too loudly in Japanese ears, while what they wish to communicate may not be heard by Americans at all.

Inadequate communications lead not just to friction in relationships but also to endless misunderstandings and misapprehensions. North America and Western Europe can be as much the mysterious Occident to Japanese as Japan is the mysterious Orient to Westerners. For example, some Japanese have seen the recent changes in American policy and the domestic turmoil as evidence that the United States is falling into complete chaos and is losing its capacity to formulate or execute any foreign policy. An extraordinarily homogeneous people themselves, they tend to overemphasize the problems of a heterogeneous society like ours and overlook the strengths and cultural richness this diversity gives us. Similarly, Americans and Europeans are prone to misinterpret Japanese developments, viewing with alarm or puzzlement what may seem perfectly natural and not particularly worrisome to those who understand Japan. The recent vogue of crediting Japanese with virtually diabolical skills of organization is but the latest of such misperceptions through the darkened glass of inadequate communications.

I have not discussed the friction and suspicion between the Japanese and the other members of the triangular community in an effort to analyze the problem fully or to pass judgment on the rights and wrongs of the situation. Nor do I mean to imply that the Security Treaty between the United States and Japan is doomed or that the two countries will become estranged. My own estimate is that the reasons for close cooperation between them are so overwhelming that they will find ways to overcome this friction and doubt. I also believe that the triangular community will survive its present difficulties and continue to develop. My purpose has merely been to show that the problems within the triangular community are not simply technical matters of making adjustments because of different rates of economic growth and changing perceptions of defense needs. They involve much more basic problems of human understanding. Behind these difficulties lie patterns of thought and action deeply entrenched by history. Technology may have forced Western Europe, North America, and Japan to form a sort of community, but the real question is whether Europeans, Americans, and Japanese are ready to live with one another in such a community.

Westerners are not far removed from their nineteenth-century certainties of racial as well as cultural superiority. This is probably truer of Western Europeans, living in a relatively tight community of Western nations deep in the Western heartland, than it is of Americans, with their somewhat broader geographic perspectives and their wider contact at home as well as abroad with other races and cultures. On the other hand, the old American dream of being the model for the world's future and the more recent postwar experience as the would-be "world policeman" and leader have perhaps made Americans more unconsciously arrogant and domineering than Europeans. Certainly in their relations with Japan, patterns of unconscious domination still survive from the American role as the supposedly all-wise mentor of a contrite Japan during the occupation and then as its benign protector, economic benefactor, and kindly big brother. Both Americans and Europeans seem to take it for granted that, to live in the same community with us, Japanese must conform to our practices and attitudes, not we to theirs. We criticize them for failing to surmount the linguistic barrier between us, without giving much thought to trying to scale it from our side. It may be that the Japanese are justified in their fear that Americans and Europeans have not come very far from the nineteenth-century concept that the world was being unified by the subordination of the rest of its peoples to Western domination or at least to Western norms.

The Japanese are equally bedeviled by their past. Japan throughout history has been perhaps the most isolated of the major countries of the world. It maintained an almost complete, even if artificial, isolation from 1639 until 1854. Its very distinctive language and extremely difficult writing system still serve to form a high cultural barrier around the country, despite Japan's global economic role. For these reasons, the Japanese have become perhaps the most homogeneous large body of people in the world and have also developed the strongest sense of "we-ness," as opposed to the "they-ness" of all other peoples. They have taken satisfaction in being "unique" and different and have derived a sense of security from the inability of others to understand Japan. In any international context, the individual Japanese tends to think of himself as first of all a Japanese, with the dignity of his whole nation resting on his shoulders. The Japanese are extremely conscious of racism in others because they are so profoundly racist themselves. These racist attitudes extend just as much to their neighbors as to distant peoples. Despite the popular phrase, "The same culture, the same race," most Japanese would be more distressed to have their daughter marry a Chinese than to marry an Occidental.

The Japanese have taken their tendency toward hierarchic social groupings at home and applied it to the world order. Their traditional society has been described as vertical rather than horizontal, being made up not so much of associations of equals as of hierarchic groupings in families, bureaucracies, businesses, schools, political parties, and every other conceivable type of organization. They tend to see the nations of the world in a similar pecking order. No people are more conscious of world ratings in GNP, sports, or any other possible way of ranking nations. If they have felt themselves subordinate to the United States, they have felt a strong sense of superiority to Asian nations. Thus the Japanese too have great difficulties in developing a feeling of equality and intimacy in a community of nations.

Because of these underlying psychological problems and the difficulty of surmounting them through better communications, the uneasiness between Japan and the other members of the triangular community constitutes a very serious crisis—perhaps the greatest crisis in international relations in the decade of the 1970's. A failure of Japan to merge more fully into the triangular community would of course not be catastrophic in this time span. The community of industrialized trading nations might with little difficulty slip back to being once again a geographically, culturally, and racially limited Atlantic community. The long-range implications of such a failure, however, are frightening. As we have seen, it would represent a slipping back on the steep slope toward the achievement of global organs of cooperation. Even more discouraging would be the fact that this failure would be precisely in the area of greatest foreseeable difficulty in the achievement of a world community—that is, along the great human fault lines of race and culture.

My whole thesis is that mankind must before long develop a true world community, embracing all nations or at least the great majority of them. The present triangular community is probably a necessary stage in the development of this larger community, but, given the exigencies of time, determined by inexorable technological advances, it can only be a very temporary stage. In the recent past, military tensions between the industrialized Communist nations and the triangular community have seemed the most serious barriers to the development of a world community. On the whole, however, these appear to be fading problems, and I believe, the development of a closer and less hazardous relationship between the industrialized Communist countries and the triangular community will not prove an insurmountable task. Much more difficult will be the inclusion of the less developed countries. This is not only because the latter constitute so much larger a part of the human race. It is even more because, while the industrialized Communist nations share a common cultural and racial background with the bulk of the countries of the triangular community, the gap between these two groups and the less developed countries, as we have seen, coincides in large part with one of the greatest cultural and racial lines of division within the human race.

The basic uneasiness we find today in Japan's relations with the Western members of the present triangular community will probably emerge on a still greater scale in the relationship between the non-Western, less developed nations, which comprise the greater part of humanity, and the industrialized Western nations. The many specific problems of military, economic, and political adjustment are likely to be severely exacerbated by a deep sense of racial and cultural differentness between these two major groupings and by a lack of understanding between them. Most of the less developed nations probably have even greater suspicions of Western nations, whether non-Communist or Communist, than do the Japanese. They may feel cultural and racial differences as strongly. They are probably even less experienced at being members of a community of nations. Certainly the inward-looking tendency of China, which is a product of its huge size and its long tradition of disdain for the outside world, is no better preparation for community life than the self-conscious Japanese sense of "uniqueness." And the difficulty of the Western nations in accepting Japan on terms of equality gives little promise that Americans and Europeans will be any more able to extend equality to much larger non-Western populations a few years hence. If we find it hard to overcome problems of this sort between the Western nations and Japan today, how can we hope for success when we face these problems on a much bigger scale with Chinese, Indians, and Africans in the not very distant future?

The present tensions in our relationship with Japan perhaps give us our best insight into what the greatest problems in building a world community are likely to be. Certainly there will be complex technological difficulties, serious economic frictions, perhaps even critical questions of military security. But much larger and more difficult than these various problems will be those of adequate communication, knowledge, and understanding, particularly across the major dividing lines between cultures and races. The development on the basis of such understanding of a sense of shared interests and common identity as members of a single world community will be even more difficult. These are the needs that most challenge education today. It is in meeting or failing to meet them that education will show whether or not it is adequate for human survival in the twenty-first century.

PART THREE
EDUCATION FOR
A WORLD COMMUNITY

1 ☮ AN OVERVIEW

The picture I have drawn of unfolding international problems and the difficulties in the way of developing a world community is admittedly sketchy and incomplete. Some of its main outlines may be seriously overdrawn. The problems we face may be less severe and the time we have in which to solve them considerably longer. Some important elements may be entirely missing and others seriously out of proportion. But for all its vagueness and uncertainty, it does serve to suggest the urgency and enormity of the problems and some of their more difficult features. I feel sure that anyone who honestly attempts to peer a generation or two ahead will perceive much more reason for despair than for easy optimism.

The question remains: What can education do about all this? Clearly, not everything. I would be the last to suggest that a world community can be developed through any single master plan, much less a plan limited to the field of education. But education certainly must be part of the effort—a crucial part, in fact. Whatever may be one's analysis of the road ahead for mankind, there can be no doubt that education faces some stupendous tasks.

Some people assume that international relations, as the term implies, involve only the relations between nations and therefore need only be the concern of governments. Government specialists, such people may feel, can adequately handle these problems. If this were correct, then the training of the limited number of experts required would be only a very specialized and limited educational undertaking. But this, of course, is quite wrong. International relations are by no means so restricted.

If a world community does materialize, it will be the product, not just of intergovernmental negotiations by a few specialists, but of a cumulative growth deriving from a myriad of diverse undertakings, each adding a gossamer strand to the ties that finally unite the world. There must, of course, be thousands of intergovernmental efforts to work out specific problems and develop more adequate organs of political cooperation. But there also must be tens of thousands of cooperative undertakings in the field of economics and in cultural and intellectual activities, and many millions of contacts between individuals which help to develop an awareness of other peoples and nations and a sense of shared interests. The politician, the bureaucrat, the international trader, the representative of the multi-national corporation, the scientist, the scholar, the concerned citizen in his local community, or the world traveler—be he athlete, performer in a rock band, teacher, college dropout, or affluent retired person—all will be taking part. Their roles in building a world community may often be unconscious but nonetheless important. Thus, not just a few government experts are involved but a very broad swath of the citizenry in a great number of fields.

Seen in this light, the role of education becomes much larger. Skills in communication and knowledge about other countries and cultures must be spread much more widely if these diverse efforts at international cooperation are to be successful and these numberless contacts meaningful. There must be many thousands of persons with truly expert knowledge about foreign areas and highly developed skills in communicating with other peoples. Beyond that, there will have to be millions more with a considerable degree of knowledge, even if below the specialist level.

The burden on education thus is a heavy one, and its role expands to a whole new dimension when we take two other factors into consideration. One is that the countries which will probably have to take the lead in the development of a world community are all democracies, and therefore the wisdom and effectiveness of the policies of their governments depend in the last analysis on the knowledge and understanding of their citizens as a whole. In other words, the bulk of the people must have some knowledge about world problems and some understanding of the necessity for global cooperation. Since such knowledge and understanding is not to be derived automatically from their experience within their respective national units, education faces a very large task indeed.

The other factor is the necessity for a large percentage of people everywhere in the world to develop a genuine sense of belonging to a world community, if such a community is ever to succeed. The tribe, the city state, the traditional empire, and later the nation state could never have functioned efficiently for long unless the people in each of these various units had felt themselves to be members of it. Similarly, the world community we must develop will never come into being or operate successfully unless the bulk of the people feel themselves to be members of a world community—that is, unless they develop a sense of world citizenship. This clearly is the biggest educational task of all, for millenniums of history have conditioned men to think in terms of smaller and more exclusive units, while suspicion and hostility toward other groups lie deep in their patterns of thought.

In order to try to come to grips more specifically with the educational needs we face in the international field, we might analyze these according to three categories, each divided into three levels. One category could be determined by the level of necessary knowledge and understanding. The uppermost level then would be expert knowledge and high skills in communication on the part of a relatively small number of specialists. Since such expert knowledge would have to cover a variety of fields of activity and a large number of different cultures and nations, even this relatively small band of experts would have to number in the tens of thousands for the United States alone. The second level would be a somewhat lesser degree of knowledge and perhaps some skills in communication among the many other persons who will be concerned in some way or other with international contacts and cooperation. The numbers involved here would certainly be in the millions. Finally, there would have to be some general understanding of world problems and a sense of world citizenship among the population as a whole.

A second three-way division of the educational problems can be made by age groupings. We are already deeply involved in international contacts but without adequate expert skills or broad enough knowledge. Much must be done at the post-school-age level to compensate for these lacks. The basic effort at developing expert knowledge and high skills of communication, however, will obviously have to come at the level of higher education, both undergraduate and graduate. So also will the development of the second level of high but less than expert knowledge. At present our colleges and universities are quite unable to meet either need adequately.

The most crucial problem, however, exists at the level of elementary and secondary education. A generalized understanding of world problems and a sense of world citizenship obviously have to be developed here, because most people never reach the level of higher education. Even in the United States, less than half of the college-age group actually enters institutions of higher learning that could reasonably be expected to take on such tasks, and in the rest of the nations that constitute the existing triangular community the numbers run from around 20 per cent in Canada and Japan to less than 10 per cent in some other countries. An even more important point is that something as basic as a sense of world citizenship is probably formed either early in life or not at all. It cannot safely be left to the college level, much less to later years.

Here we get back to the problem of the six-year-olds who are just starting their formal schooling. They will be the leaders and average citizens of the early twenty-first century. Their generation will have to have far more expert skills and much broader knowledge about the outside world than the present adult generation, and beyond this they will have to have a much stronger sense of world citizenship if there is to be much chance for human survival. The twenty-first century may seem a long way off, but, as we have seen, in terms of educational preparation it is already here.

The third category of our analysis is the relative importance and urgency in the various regions of the world of developing the sort of international education we are discussing. Here the differences are marked, and a general three-way division seems reasonable between what I have called the three angles of the great human triangle—that is, the existing triangular community of industrialized, trading nations, the industrialized Communist nations, and the less developed countries.

Clearly, the countries of the existing triangular community are in the most urgent need of developing an international approach to education. They collectively dominate global trade and most other international contacts, and they have by far the largest influence on what happens in the world. Since they exercise the greatest power, their ignorance and lack of skills in international relations are especially dangerous. Since they have the broadest and deepest relations with other parts of the world, they in particular need the requisite knowledge and skills to handle these relations successfully.

Within the triangular community, one might say that the richer and more powerful a country is and the greater its involvement in wide international relationships, the greater the urgency that it develop a more international approach to education. According to these criteria, the need would be greatest of all in the United States, which has close to a third of the world's wealth and exercises a broader influence than any other nation. Next perhaps might come Japan, which is rising so rapidly as a world economic power but has been so isolated throughout history, has a strong sense of separateness from the rest of the world, and is hampered in all its international contacts by high linguistic barriers. The need, however, is great in all the countries of the triangular community —and also in the many other countries which, through rapid industrial development and extensive international trade, are starting to become members of this community.

The industrialized Communist nations, with their restricted foreign contacts and limited international trade, may face a less urgent problem. Certainly it is a different one from that of the countries of the triangular community. Their political systems do not depend in the same way on popular understanding expressed through elections. Their need for expert knowledge and skills in communication is far less generalized, though actually the Soviet Union has done notably well in one aspect of international communication—the teaching of foreign languages. Their traditional concept of a world dictatorship of the proletariat is a somewhat different and, I believe, decidedly less realistic ideal than the concept of world citizenship. In any case, many of the educational requirements we are considering here will not be critical in these countries until they develop broader international contacts and have become more integrated into the world economy. If they progress in these directions, as I believe they will, their needs in international education will become more like those of the countries of the triangular community; but this is a supposition about the future, not the present.

In the less developed countries, too, the needs in international education are different and in some ways less pressing. Many of these countries are still in the process of developing their own national identities and will therefore have little enthusiasm for complicating this task by stressing world citizenship. Nor is the development of expert or even generalized knowledge about many distant areas an urgent need for them, because they have little present contact with these areas and no influence. They also often lack an adequate supply of well-educated citizens and would see little point in diverting those they do have to specialized study of areas still not important to them. Furthermore, not many of the less developed countries are democracies in which the government's foreign policies really depend on wide popular understanding.

In time, as the less developed countries do industrialize and become more integrated into the world community, their needs in international education will more closely parallel those of the nations of the triangular community, but that may still be some years off. In the meantime, their requirements in this field are more restricted, though still very important. They are, I believe, basically two: to produce adequate skills in communication with the outside world and to develop adequate knowledge about those specific countries with which they do have or are likely soon to have significant contacts. Unfortunately, their records in meeting even these limited needs are in many cases quite unsatisfactory.

The schools in a less developed nation usually teach little if anything about even near neighbors. Its educational system is likely to have been derived from that of the former colonial administration, which very probably included little enough about the country itself, much less about neighboring regions that might then have been in the empires of other colonial powers. In correcting this situation, post-independence educators have understandably emphasized instruction about their own country and have not wished to dilute this with material on other countries, however close geographically or culturally. The net result has commonly been a serious lack of knowledge about nearby lands with which the country in question inevitably will have intimate relations and may in fact be trying to form a regional community. All too often, old traditions of suspicion and hostility toward neighboring peoples have been permitted to continue uncorrected.

While the colonial educational legacy may have left a strong residue of study about the former colonial power, this is likely to concern the past of that country rather than its present conditions. Thus, students in former British colonies may learn quite a bit about Shakespeare or the times of William the Conqueror, Elizabeth I, and Victoria, but little about postwar British politics, society, and culture. I well remember a professor in a North Indian city complaining to me a few years ago that his children were learning the names of the rivers of Devon, which are mere rivulets by Indian standards and obviously of little interest to anyone who does not live in Devon.

A more serious problem is that the colonial educational legacy is likely to have left little in it concerning other industrialized areas that in the meantime may have become even more important to that particular country than is the former colonial power. Thus, the school-children of the Indian subcontinent, while being taught perhaps too much about the geography of England and its pre-twentieth-century history, learn next to nothing about the United States or Japan, which may loom larger in their future. Similarly, the United States figures much in the textbooks of students in the Philippines, but Japan not at all, except as an enemy in World War II.

It is more difficult to generalize about the record of the less developed countries in teaching skills in international communication. This for the most part means competence in foreign languages, usually English, which has become overwhelmingly the language of international communication. The one significant exception is the so-called Francophone countries of Africa, which were once part of the French or Belgian empires. English unfortunately is by no means the ideal choice. It has a more complex and irregular grammar than many languages, a relatively difficult set of sounds, and an absolutely absurd system of spelling, giving it one of the worst writing systems among the alphabetically written languages. A planned world order would have used some artificially developed language like Esperanto or at least a more sensibly written language like Spanish. But, as we have seen, human institutions usually defy planning. For a number of reasons—the nineteenth-century British Empire, the English-speaking lands that grew up overseas in North America and Oceania, and the dominant role of the United States ever since World War II— English has become and is likely to remain the chief language of international communication.

The colonial educational heritage has often left relatively high standards in the teaching of a foreign language. In this regard the former colonial lands have a linguistic advantage over such countries as China, Japan, and Korea, which, unlike most Western nations, do not speak any of the present international languages or a tongue related to them and, unlike most less developed nations, do not have a colonial past that injected an international language deeply into their societies and educational systems. But even in some of those countries that did derive this linguistic benefit from their colonial past, there has been a distressing falling off in recent years in skills in the use of an international language. In some cases, this has been due to the difficulties encountered in the transition to independence or to a sudden expansion of formal education, which resulted in the lowering of standards. In other cases, the effort to strengthen national identity through a newly established national language in a multi-language state has led to a corresponding de-emphasis on foreign language skills. India and the Philippines may be cases in point. While conditions vary greatly, most less developed countries, strictly in their own immediate interests, need to improve their foreign language skills.

We have seen that the specific needs in the field of international education and their urgency vary considerably among the three groups of countries I have described as the great triangle of humanity. In the remaining chapters, I shall limit my focus to the needs in the countries of the triangular community of industrialized, trading nations, in which the urgency is greatest. I shall discuss these needs basically in terms of the American educational system and American social conditions. This is because I would probably lose both myself and the reader in encyclopedic detail if I were to attempt to express these needs in terms of the specific educational systems and societies of each of the countries in this community. But the general principles, I believe, apply to all and will in time also apply to a large extent to the industrialized Communist nations and those of the less developed regions.

2 ☙ KNOWLEDGE
AND UNDERSTANDING

No one would deny the necessity for a great deal more specialized knowledge about other nations on the part of experts, broader skills in communicating across linguistic and cultural lines, and a much wider understanding of international problems on the part of the general public. In almost every aspect of international relations our knowledge and understanding are deficient even for our present needs, to say nothing of the future which is bearing down on us at such alarming speed. This is all so obvious and has been so often stated that it hardly needs exposition again here. But for the sake of balance, I might briefly present some illustrations of these needs and outline some approaches to meeting them, before going on to the main objective of this book, which is a consideration of the problem of building a sense of world citizenship.

The one field in which we have developed a great deal of expert knowledge about foreign countries is the military. This is not surprising in view of our concentration on the balance of power and military defense. The result has been a serious imbalance between the attention we pay to military matters and the countries that seem to present a strategic threat on the one hand and nonmilitary matters and the countries that do not seem menacing on the other. A good example is the trifling attention we have devoted to the countries of the Indian subcontinent as compared with China, though the difference between the two areas is by no means that great in population, in overall contacts with us, or in their probable impact on the future of the world.

An example of a different sort can be drawn from the disproportionate emphasis we have placed on our military contacts with Japan and the development of military knowledge about that country, even though the nonmilitary aspects of our relations are incomparably greater. We have tended to let the military tail wag the dog. Let me cite an illustration from my experience at the American Embassy in Tokyo. Except for overall policy direction, our military relationship with Japan was handled for the most part through the three military services themselves and their military commands in Japan. The services, however, also saw fit to maintain attaché offices at the embassy, which in aggregate American personnel were considerably larger than the economic and commercial staffs, even though the latter served as the governmental contact point in a tremendous economic relationship between the two countries that far overshadowed the military. The armed services also took pains to prepare their men for their tasks much better than did the economic branches of our government. The military and naval officers attached to the embassy were in most cases given a year of Japanese language study, followed by a year of service connected with Japan in the Pentagon, before they were sent to Tokyo. The economic and commercial officers by contrast were lucky if they had had any previous contact with Japanese affairs.

I am not suggesting that our military expertise on other countries is greater than it need be, but rather that our nonmilitary expertise is seriously deficient. Even in what have been assumed to be military problems, the other neglected aspects may be the more important. Certainly in our defense relationship with Japan, psychological and cultural problems have been much more thorny than military matters. We got into our disastrous war in Vietnam not because of a lack of military intelligence but because of ignorance about political realities and psychological attitudes. The failures in prosecuting this war may have been in part military, but they were much more political, economic, social, and psychological. We should not be surprised at this. There was virtually no expert knowledge on Vietnam in any of these fields for our leaders to call on, even if they had seen the need to do so.

Thus our knowledge of the nonmilitary fields of activity in other countries is seriously inadequate even when viewed as ancillary to military problems. The deficiency becomes much worse when we realize that man's fate is likely to be determined less by military matters than by economic and other nonmilitary relations between nations and by their capacity to cooperate with one another to meet global problems. Seen in this light, the needs for expert knowledge about all parts of the world seem almost unlimited and certainly far beyond what we have today.

The Department of State is commonly made the

whipping boy for our failures in foreign relations, but this is unfair. It has valiantly attempted to develop some of the expert knowledge the United States needs, but it faces insurmountable obstacles raised by the government as a whole and the electorate behind it. The Department's budget is entirely inadequate for the purpose. Because military expenditures are so astronomically high, other government expenditures must be kept down. The budget of the State Department can be kept particularly low because it lacks the built-in voter clientele of the other departments of government, which provides them with political clout for their budgetary requests. The proverbial observer from outer space, seeing the huge discrepancy between the capacities of our military for worldwide activities of every sort and the shoestring operation of the Department of State, might well conclude that the State Department is only a minor service organ for the military, designed to cater to its political needs.

The Department of State has built up small corps of experts in a few areas of special importance that also have languages of particular difficulty, such as Russia, the Arab world, China, and Japan. It has not been able, however, to develop comparable corps of experts in most other fields. The service is too small and underfinanced to support many experts even in countries which have loomed as large to the United States as Korea and Vietnam or for relatively large countries like Indonesia, Brazil, and Nigeria, to say nothing of the many smaller states. Even in the areas where experts have been trained, they are insufficient and are not always well used. Promotion usually comes for more generalized activities, so the expert is likely to find himself frozen at a relatively low level, where he faces mandatory early retirement, or else he gravitates into being a generalist who may lose some of his expert knowledge and skills. There should be ample room in the system for both specialists and generalists, because both are needed.

We would regard with pity and some contempt a foreign ambassador or lesser diplomat in Washington who could neither speak English nor read the *Washington Post*. An American ambassador in Korea who does not speak and read Korean or an American Embassy officer in Cairo who knows little or no Arabic should be considered equally incompetent. There is no reason why a country like the United States should be satisfied with that sort of third-rate service in a field of activity that is so crucial to our nation and to mankind's future.

While the Department of State should be given credit for at least trying, the same cannot always be said for the other civilian branches of government. The Treasury and Commerce Departments have vital economic dealings with the rest of the world but have made little effort to develop the necessary knowledge about the political and psychological problems that make these dealings so difficult. The result is a continual running battle between the economic branches of government and the Department of State, which has more awareness of these problems. Some other departments of our government also have dealings with foreign areas, and these will undoubtedly increase in size and complexity, but they have done next to nothing to prepare for such responsibilities.

The need for more expert knowledge at the governmental level may be obvious, but the corresponding need in business is not generally recognized. Most corporations active overseas, while realizing the necessity for having specialists in their technical fields of activity, have seen little need for experts in their geographic areas of operation. They expect their promising young executives to pick up sufficient knowledge about local conditions through service in the field and to acquire whatever other knowledge and skills are needed by hiring office help on the spot. This approach has worked after a fashion in the past, but it is basically short-sighted and is already beginning to put American business abroad into a sluggish competitive position. As economic relations become larger and more intimate, which they inevitably will, and as old patterns of domination and patronage give way to new perceptions of equality and interdependence in the international community, the businessman engaged in foreign operations will undoubtedly have to develop a great deal more knowledge of the economy and politics of the country with which he is dealing and a deeper understanding of the life and psychology of its people. To do this, he will probably have to know the language in which they normally think and communicate. In other words, he will have to go halfway to meet these people on their own terms and in their own language and not expect them always to come all the way to meet him on his terms and in his language.

Corporation executives may object that they cannot find persons with "area knowledge" who also make good businessmen. The problem, however, is that they have not sought this combination of talents. Since they have not valued "area knowledge," those looking toward careers in overseas business or already started on such careers have seen no reason to devote their energies to developing such skills. As is well known, supply and demand are closely related. If corporations recognized their need for men with "area knowledge," they would find adequate numbers of young persons with such knowledge wishing to enter on careers in business and also young executives already on their rolls who would be ready to develop this "second string to their bow."

Much the same thing could be said about the smaller but vitally important field of the mass media—the television networks, the great newspapers and wire services, and the major magazines. For one thing, the mass media attempt little coverage of the non-Western world and, beyond that, most of what they do is carried out by inadequately trained persons. A foreign correspondent in the United States who knew little or no English and only a smattering about American history and society would be a professional cripple. But we have often been satisfied with American correspondents in non-Western countries who did not know the local language and had little understanding of the history or culture of the area.

It is unlikely that the American mass media would send correspondents to France who knew no French and were ignorant of French history and culture, but until quite recently they felt no compunction about sending comparably uninformed correspondents to Japan. Yet a foreign correspondent's need for language skills and specialized knowledge is greater in Japan than in France, since Japan is a far more difficult country for an untutored American to understand, and only a tiny percentage of Japanese leaders, as compared to French leaders, are able to speak in English. Of late the preparation of American correspondents in Japan has improved, but it remains distressingly low in much of the rest of the non-Western world. A correspondent in New York from Japan or some other non-Western country who could not speak English or read the New York Times and had little knowledge of American history, society, and culture would be considered an absurdity. That the reverse is not taken for granted is a clear example of continuing cultural arrogance and the tardiness of our adjustment to the world in which we now live.

One could go on almost ad nauseam with examples of the need for more expert knowledge. But the question remains how this need can be filled. Clearly, the response must be large and well-organized, but it is by no means beyond our capabilities. Much of the necessary expert knowledge can be provided through specialized training programs for those selected for international service, as is already done by the Department of State and the armed services. But the bulk of the effort should probably be somewhat broader in focus. This sort of training can be best accomplished at the undergraduate and graduate levels in colleges and universities, with further and more specialized training provided as needed and, whenever possible, in the geographic area under study. A good start, in this sort of training has already been made in some fields. All that is needed is to strengthen what exists and greatly broaden the coverage.

In the case of our cultural cousins, such as the countries of Western Europe, our manifold and close relations, together with the emphasis on these countries and their languages in our traditional educational system, may be adequate to produce the necessary experts; but for the other parts of the world special efforts are required. This would include both Latin America and the Communist countries of East Europe, which though culturally and linguistically related to us, present special problems of understanding. The need is even greater for regions of sharply different cultural background and with languages that fall outside the Indo-European family.

For some of the major countries or cultures, there are already a number of well-established research and training centers capable of producing real specialists. This is notably true in the Russian, Chinese, and Japanese fields. It is much less the case for other major areas, such as India, the Arab countries, Africa, and Latin America. But even in the better established fields there is need for considerable expansion. Existing centers need strengthening in teaching personnel and fellowship funds; in some cases more centers should be established; and all of the centers require special governmental support to maintain an adequate library foundation for advanced scholarship and the research activities that must accompany this sort of training.

The largest problem, however, is in the field of the middle-sized or small national or cultural unit. The United States is so large and rich a country and its relations with all parts of the world are so important that it must have expert knowledge about every part of the globe. There should be at least one center of research and training for every nation of average size and each grouping of smaller countries. But such centers, though national necessities, are likely to be considered superfluous luxuries by individual universities. It may be beyond their means to develop adequate centers for even such relatively large units as Nigeria, Egypt, Turkey, Thailand, or Colombia, let alone such smaller units as Paraguay, Uganda, Yemen, or Ceylon.

The problem of ensuring that there are adequate centers of training and research dealing with all parts of the world is obviously a responsibility of the federal government. The best place to create them would probably be at those universities which could buttress the work at these centers by comparable activities in closely related fields. The total costs would be small when measured against the money poured into fields of military research and development that have only a very small chance of proving of even theoretical use and still less chance of ever being employed. Such expert knowledge by contrast would be of unquestionable and possibly crucial use.

As I have frequently emphasized, skill in communication is a major part of successful international relations. Clearly our diplomats, other government experts, foreign correspondents, and some businessmen need to master foreign languages. Some may assume, however, that except for such specialists, the responsibility in this field falls on those nations which, unlike us, have the misfortune not to speak our language, which has become the chief medium of international communication.

To some extent this is true. Others do bear a far heavier linguistic burden than we. Non-English-speaking

Europeans have made great efforts and done extremely well in learning English, and often other foreign European tongues as well. As we have seen, many of the other countries of the world, because of a colonial past, have English or French deeply built into their educational systems. Some countries, however, are in more trouble.

The Japanese, for example, must meet all the rest of the world primarily through a language that is very difficult for them to master because of the radically different structure of their language and its very limited phonetic system. Since they have massive economic involvements throughout the world, they have greater needs for skill in communication than do most nations. But they have permitted antiquated teaching methods and an undertrained staff of English language teachers to vitiate the six years of formal English instruction most Japanese youths receive. The students' efforts are often enormous but the results meager. Clearly, a country like Japan faces a major problem in developing skills in international communication commensurate with its needs. Until it does so, it will be unnecessarily damaging its own immediate interests and also limiting the very great contribution to the development of a world community that Japan could make because of its tremendous economic power and great abilities in other fields.

To say that other countries have larger burdens in the field of communication than does the United States, however, does not imply that we have none. It is true that our dealings with the rest of the world will be basically in English, but this does not mean that, except for the occasional specialist, Americans need have no foreign language skills at all. It would be most unwise for us to fall such victims to cultural smugness and linguistic laziness that we made no effort to bridge the language gap from our side. If we remain bound by the limitations of our own language, it will mean that only we will lack the deeper insights into foreign cultures that knowledge of other languages permits. It will mean that only we fall into the common human prejudice of believing that another person's mispronunciations and clumsiness in the use of our language are a sign of mental inferiority. We may even create in our minds a cultural pecking order to substitute for the old Western–non-Western one—that is, a ranking system which puts smooth native speakers of English above uncouth foreign speakers of the language. In a shrinking world of growing interdependence, we obviously need more foreign language skills than we now have. Seen in this light, the somewhat precipitous decline in the study of foreign languages throughout the American educational system is a matter of grave concern, running as it does against the obvious needs of the future.

The problem of language teaching brings us to the broader problem of developing, among a large part of the American public, enough understanding of foreign nations and international relations to give this country a reasonably informed and intelligent voting public. Language study is one facet of this problem, but a larger aspect is knowledge about other societies and their histories, cultures, and attitudes.

Knowledge of this sort can be developed in a number of ways. In view of the deficiencies of our traditional educational system and the urgent need for more knowledge and understanding now, some of the effort must be at the level of adult education. Residence and travel abroad, if properly approached, can contribute a great deal. Organizations such as the Foreign Policy Association and various local Councils on World Affairs can play an important role. Public lectures are useful. The mass media and book publishers have a great responsibility. One particular need is illustrated by the present one-way flow of communication between ourselves and the Japanese. The Japanese annually publish thousands of translations of foreign books and articles, primarily from the United States and Western Europe. The reverse flow of translations is only a tiny trickle. While Japanese comment extensively on American views of the world and of Japan, as these appear in print, we remain largely unaware of their views on the world situation or on us. They in turn get no feedback from us about the views they have expressed and we no feedback on their assessment of our views. This is not real communication. There is no dialogue in the sense of an exchange of ideas.

Granted the need for adult educational efforts, the main task of preparing an informed and understanding public will still fall to formal education. Some of this task should be undertaken at the secondary or even elementary levels—an aspect of the problems I discuss more fully in the next chapter. But however well the elementary and secondary schools perform in this regard, much of the burden for this sort of instruction will fall on undergraduate education in the colleges, when the student is better prepared for a broader, more sophisticated encounter with other cultures.

There may be enough in our traditional educational system to give the average college student at least a little understanding of our close cultural cousins, but I am not at all sure even of this. Most instruction in secondary or higher education on the countries of Western Europe is on their past histories and cultural accomplishments, not on their present conditions; and there has been a marked decline in recent years even in the amount of European history taught at both the secondary and college levels. Moreover, there are some curious blind spots in our educational coverage. For example, Canada, our closest cultural cousin and biggest trading partner by a wide margin, is almost completely overlooked. It is so close and seems so familiar that Americans may feel it requires no special attention in our educational system. This situation, however, has probably contributed to what Canadians often feel to be a peculiar American insensitivity to Canada, which in turn has helped produce an entirely unnecessary uneasiness in relations between the two countries.

The major problem, however, as in the development of expert knowledge, concerns the less familiar areas of Latin America, Eastern Europe, and the various cultural divisions of the non-Western world. The average college student obviously could not be expected to become conversant with the problems and attitudes of all these areas. But if he is to be a responsible citizen, he should acquire some awareness of the problems of international relations through acquaintance with at least one of the major nations or cultural regions of the less familiar parts of the world. I do not mean to suggest that some knowledge of the culture and current problems of India will serve as an Open Sesame to an understanding of Latin America or Africa, but it would prepare one to approach these other areas with a little more perception and sympathy.

The freshman entering college this year will be a working member of society roughly from around 1980 until the year 2020 and may remain a voting member of society some decades longer. It is hard to predict exactly what knowledge and skills will be necessary for him over this long period of time, but undoubtedly he should have a great deal more understanding of the outside world than past generations have had. Certainly it is not too much to ask of him to acquire some knowledge of at least one other culture than his own. This is only a minimal demand in terms of the needs of a democratic society in the stage of history into which our scientific skills are forcing us.

To meet this need, I believe that all institutions of higher education, or at least every liberal arts program, should offer competent instruction on at least one of the major countries or cultural areas outside our own cultural community, and that all college students should be encouraged or possibly required to take a course or two in such a field. It may seem a tall order for some small and weak institutions to provide the requisite instruction in a different cultural area, but in the world we now live in, instruction of this sort should be regarded as being as basic a part of a liberal arts program as such old standbys as English, history, or mathematics. Actually, the goal outlined above is much closer to achievement than many people realize. Virtually all institutions of any distinction offer instruction in at least one area of different culture, and the concept that some study of such an area should be mandatory is beginning to spread.

Some people may agree that an introduction to a different culture should be made part of all undergraduate education but might at the same time feel that such studies would not make an appropriate undergraduate major or field of concentration. This, I believe, is a mistaken view. A broad examination of a radically different culture, together with some study of its language, would seem to me a very suitable undergraduate major. The role of a liberal arts education is usually considered three-fold: to give the student a general preparation for later life; to give him a chance to discover where his major interests may lie; or to give him a preprofessional background for postgraduate training in his already determined career. A major in the study of a different cultural area fits all three functions. For some, it can be preprofessional preparation for graduate training as a specialist in one of these areas. As we have seen, there will undoubtedly be a growing demand for such expert knowledge. For those still trying to discover themselves and their interests, such a major should prove as stimulating and open up as many different possible areas for further exploration as would a more traditional major, such as one in political science, biology, or French literature. For those seeking merely a general preparation for life, few majors would be more relevant. International problems will be crucial to man's survival, and the mirror of a different culture can show our own society and perhaps ourselves individually in a revealing new light.

In conclusion, it can be said that adequate expert knowledge about the rest of the world and a public reasonably informed on foreign affairs are already well-recognized needs, and considerable progress has been made toward achieving them. The problem is simply to expand and improve what we have. The task is probably greater than most people realize, because the acceleration of change means rapidly increasing requirements. We could, in terms of our presently perceived needs, set targets to be met within a decade and achieve these goals, only to find ourselves as far behind in meeting the real needs as we are today. But the task in these fields is clearly within our capacities. The same may not be true of the problem of developing a sense of world citizenship. This is an undertaking of entirely different magnitude, which will require some fresh approaches and tremendous new efforts.

3 ✿ WORLD CITIZENSHIP

The very concept of world citizenship may not be a generally accepted ideal. Some may regard it as virtually treasonable to national interests. Others may pay it lip service but no more. The goal itself may seem fuzzy. There are few serious efforts to achieve it, and none on a significant scale. And yet to have much meaning, a sense of world citizenship cannot be limited just to a few experts or even to the better informed citizens. It must be spread throughout the whole population. And the period within which this must be done may be very short. In the case of the internationally more isolated and less influential countries, there may still be considerable time; but for countries like the United States, Japan, and those of Western Europe, which are already deeply involved in worldwide relationships and exert global influence, there is no time to waste. It is probably imperative for us to make great strides in this direction by the early twenty-first century, which is just around the corner, in view of the slowness of the educational process. The task is a huge one, calling for extensive exploratory efforts, the development of new techniques, and very probably a considerable restructuring of some aspects of our educational system.

We first might try to clarify what the goal is. I shall not repeat the arguments about the increasing complexity and intimacy of international relations throughout the world and the growing interdependence of all mankind, bound together now in a common fate. There is no denying the emerging "one world" and the need for a world community. My argument is that such a community cannot be built simply on the intellectual realization of its necessity and the organs of international cooperation this realization makes possible. Both of these are, of course, needed, but so also is an emotional awareness of shared interests and common identity as human beings. It is this last key element that I have called a sense of world citizenship.

The nation state has its many practical reasons for existence and its complex organs of cooperation, but to make it an effective unit of action it has also required an emotional component—the sense of "we Frenchmen," or "we Americans," or "we Japanese." The same was true of the smaller units before the nation state. There clearly had to be a sense of "we Venetians," "we Franks," "we Athenians," "we Persians," "we men of Ur," "we Incas," or "we Iroquois." "We world citizens" may sound flat by comparison. Change it to "we human beings," and it still does not conjure up the enemy "they" groups that have helped give the "we" groups of the past solidarity and fervor. The enemy is not alien Martians but ourselves. It is our own capacity for self-destruction. But the need for an emotional sense of common identity is the same. Without it, a world community would probably founder.

I should make clear that I am not talking about the creation of a world government. If mankind does survive through the development of a genuine world community, this community will evolve the organs of cooperation it requires. It seems improbable to me that these organs, at least initially, will take the form of a world parliament and international bureaucracy along the lines of the United Nations. They will more likely resemble the various consultative and regulatory bodies of the European Community, or such groupings as the O.E.C.D. in the triangular community, or the many existing bodies for worldwide cooperation in technical matters that cluster around the United Nations. But in any case, the growth of organs of international cooperation is an entirely different matter from the development of a sense of world citizenship. They would be the rational outgrowth of a world community, while a sense of world citizenship is the emotional prerequisite for such a community to come into being.

The sense of world citizenship need not and should not replace a sense of national identity or a feeling of loyalty to the still smaller groupings within society. The latter have succeeded quite well in co-existing with the nation state. A good example is the strong state pride in the United States, sometimes symbolized by fierce rivalries between the football teams of state universities. Time after time in history, the smaller group—the family, the tribe, the city state—has been forced by changing conditions to subordinate its hitherto exclusive sense of self to a broader unit of overarching common interests, though without losing its own identity in the process. This is what is required once more, but on a global scale. The European Community affords an example of how there can be co-existence at this higher level. In Western

Europe, national pride remains strong but national rivalries are gradually being subordinated to a broader sense of common identity and common interests.

The distinction between an emotional sense of unity and an intellectual awareness of its necessity is very great. A good illustration is afforded by the socialist and labor movements at the time of World War I. There was much conviction in those circles at that time that laboring men in all countries shared common interests which basically ran counter to the policies of their respective governments, but when the war came these intellectual attitudes proved to be no more than sandcastles swept away by the tides of nationalistic fervor. Intellectual convictions about shared interests among nations are likely to suffer the same fate today if there is no emotional sense of common identity.

Some people may feel that ideological differences are the major and possibly insuperable barriers to the achievement of a sense of world citizenship. I would not deny that they do form a great impediment, but it seems to me they are far from insuperable and are probably not the biggest difficulty we face. As has often been pointed out, there appears to be considerable convergence in reality, even if not in rhetoric, between the industrialized Communist states and the industrialized democratic nations—or call them socialist and capitalist, if you wish to stress economic rather than political systems. The former show some signs of becoming less fully controlled economically, socially, and even politically, and somewhat less autarkic in their economies. The latter continue a steady drift toward what is called a welfare society, which has many resemblances to the Communist and socialist ideals. But whether convergence is happening or not, the important point is that a world community can consist of very dissimilar political, social, and economic units. The apparent acceptance of the concept of co-existence in the Soviet Union and the lessening of the "cold war" mentality on both sides shows that there is a growing realization of this fact in both groups of countries and a greater appreciation that their common interests transcend political and economic differences.

A much more serious problem, I believe, is the feeling of differentness—the sense of unbridgeable alienness—between races and still more between cultures of radically different background. In actuality, racial barriers to cooperation are much less substantial than those between different economic, social, and political systems. Race in fact need be no barrier at all, and even cultural differences could be accommodated with ease in a world community. The problem is basically emotional—the feeling that others are too different from us to be really part of the same "we" group. The Britisher may mutter "poor devils" over the massacre or oppression of some group in Africa but may feel less actual concern than he does about the "humane" treatment of dogs and horses. Does the Japanese have much fellow feeling for the Arab, or the American for the citizens of Bangladesh, the "international basket case," as they have been called? I have discussed at some length the problem between Japan and the Western members of the triangular community because it illustrates this point, though at a more sophisticated and more immediately crucial level.

The importance of the emotional aspect of a sense of

world citizenship and the great difficulties in interracial and intercultural relations are points I may feel with particular keenness because of my own special background. Despite an entirely traditional American heritage and education, the fact that I spent most of my childhood in Japan gave me a dual perspective on the world. I was proud to be an American but also proud of my "home town," Tokyo. At a time when the European empires and Western domination of the world were accepted by most Westerners without question, I had a strong emotional bias against both. British police in Hong Kong or Dutch officials in Indonesia seemed to me incongruous and wrong—or, to use the modern rhetoric, "immoral." When I discovered Japanese colonialism in Korea and American domination in the Philippines and Latin America, I should add, I found them equally distasteful.

I still find myself sensitive to continued Western arrogance, however unconscious it may be, and sharply aware of the distinction between intellectual perceptions of the need for a sense of world citizenship and a deep emotional commitment to it. Many plead for it intellectually without feeling it emotionally. The result too often is a cold intellectuality that can be chilling to any real sense of fellow feeling. Others slip back to Rousseau's naïve concept of the "noble savage," accepting, for example, with patronizing good will a simplistic image of Chinese and Vietnamese peasants as beautiful primitives devoted in a simple-minded way to their "good earth" and narrow local groupings. Or again they develop well-meaning but patronizing enthusiasms—"I just love your native dances"—when the real concern of the other person, whether or not he too loves the "native dances," is over levels of literacy, new industries, or the terms of trade. "Native dances" are part of the world's cultural riches, but those that dance them have more serious ambitions than to add exotic color to other people's lives. No one wants to live in a cultural game preserve. Nothing could be more arrogant than the well-meant advice sometimes given to people in preindustrial societies to beware of the miseries of affluence.

Many things can contribute to building a sense of world citizenship. The development of expert knowledge and the growth of a reasonably informed and sympathetic citizenry both help. The myriad of contacts in the economic and cultural fields may be even more important, because they all involve shared interests. Travel abroad is, of course, important, though not the brief, casual trip in which the tourist first peers at the wild animals in Kenya and then at the tamer fauna in Kashmir or Bali. To be of value, travel must go deeper than the tourist level. Study, teaching, the pursuit of a hobby, or simply business can all help one get below the surface of international hotels, sycophantic guides, haggling shopkeepers, and picture postcard exotica. Only then will one really meet people and have some chance to develop a sense of fellow feeling.

I have noticed a direct correlation between age and the relevance of an experience abroad. One could posit the rule that, except for very small children, the younger the traveler or resident abroad, the more likely he is to establish real contacts with the local people and develop a sense of shared human identity and interests. Perhaps this situation is related to the fact that the younger the person is, the greater his capacity to absorb foreign languages. But there seems much more to it than just greater linguistic ability. Less established patterns of thought and conduct and a greater openness of mind may be more important. In any case, it seems to me a demonstrable fact that the high-school student who studies abroad is likely to be more basically influenced by his experience than is the college undergraduate, and the undergraduate similarly more influenced than the graduate student, even though the latter may be better prepared scholastically for the experience and more purposeful in his efforts.

I have been particularly struck by the impact of a year or even a summer of study abroad on students at the high-school level. I am, of course, not referring to those confined to the golden ghettos and schools of American military enclaves or similar national groupings. I have in mind rather the exchange student who lives with a local family and attends school or a joint summer program with a member of that family of corresponding age. Below the high-school age level, such student exchanges may encounter too many difficulties to be worth trying, and between countries of markedly different living standards they may present serious problems. But from my own personal observation I know that they have been vastly successful in developing a sense of shared human identity even between countries like the United States and Japan, which are separated by a high language barrier and a broad cultural gap. This is as true for Japanese participants as for Americans. Here certainly is one very important technique in attempting to build a sense of world citizenship.

The factor of age in the impact of a foreign experience suggests the reverse side of the familiar adage that old dogs cannot learn new tricks. "Tricks," of course, is not the right word in this case. Old human dogs do pick up new skills and tricks, but they do not easily acquire new "gut feelings," and this is what we are really talking about. The intellectual acceptance of the world community may be as easy for the old as for the young, and they can work as hard and enthusiastically for its achievement. But they are much less likely to learn to really feel it.

For young and old alike, however, residence and study abroad will no doubt remain the privilege of the few, not the experience of the majority. Such an approach, no matter how effective, can only be part of the answer to the problem. The basic task in building a sense of world citizenship inevitably falls on the education of the young within their own countries, particularly on education in the narrow sense of schooling. Here we get back to our six year old, who will start school this year but not be a voting citizen for another twelve years or a leader until the early twenty-first century. The major effort in creating a sense of world citizenship must be aimed at him. It will have to be basically a generational change in attitudes, as, I believe, most great changes are. It will also have to be achieved primarily through elementary and secondary education, because this is the best way to reach the majority of the people in any nation and that is the age at which most basic feelings are formed. Unfortunately, the effort will undoubtedly be an uphill battle—against long-established patterns of education, against indoctrination in conflicting attitudes both at home and throughout society, and against a basic adult skepticism, made perhaps more dangerous because it is concealed by a thin veneer of lip service.

There have been many efforts in recent years to put into the content of elementary and secondary education a great deal more about foreign nations and different cultures. These range from well-developed programs at the sixth- or seventh-year level on selected foreign nations or non-Western cultures to quite advanced study at the eleventh- or twelfth-year level of the history and culture of some foreign country, such as China or Japan, and sometimes even its language. Such admirable beginnings should be expanded further and spread to other school systems. They help develop the awareness of the outside world and the understanding of it that the intelligent voter needs. And they no doubt inspire some students to pursue these subjects further in college. If well taught, such programs and courses can also stimulate a sense of world citizenship.

Our present efforts along these lines, however, are not adequate to meet the needs of the situation. As I pointed out at the start, they are not widely enough spread, being found for the most part only in the more affluent and more urbanized parts of the country. They also are often improperly focused. Programs of study about other countries and cultures sometimes are structured to teach how others differ from us, rather than how they are like us and share common interests and a common fate. It is natural in such programs to select countries of contrasting types and to stress in each the points of difference from us.

Such differences can be both strikingly obvious and intrinsically interesting. Underlying human similarities, by comparison, might be too simple and dull to catch the child's attention, while the concept of shared interests in the stage of history we are now entering may be too complex and abstract to be grasped at this age level.

If poorly taught, courses of this sort, while still serving to show the diversity and complexity of the world, could do more harm than good so far as the development of a sense of world citizenship is concerned. There is always the temptation to stress what seems to us exotic. Chinese are not like you and me—and other normal people, is what is implied—who eat with knives, forks, and spoons. They eat with funny little sticks called chopsticks. They don't write with an alphabet but with curious picture-like symbols—and, believe it or not, not from left to right (except they really do in China today), but from top to bottom. Still worse is the all too frequent emphasis put on small, unusual groups like the Eskimos to represent the outside world. There may no longer be any Eskimos who live in igloos and there never were many, but a child can all too easily develop the picture of an outside world where people live in ice houses, write backwards, and do other quaint but obviously irrational things. This may make them seem interesting but hardly members of the same community to which he belongs. I wonder if we have really got much beyond the nursery rhyme of an earlier generation:

> Little Indian, Sioux or Crow,
> Little frosty Eskimo,
> Little Turk or Japanee,
> O! don't you wish that you were me? . . .

You have curious things to eat,
I am fed on proper meat;
You must dwell beyond the foam,
But I am safe and live at home.*

Even assuming that the types of courses we are discussing are taught well and spread widely in the school system, they will not adequately develop a sense of world citizenship for another, more basic reason. They are merely additional or even peripheral to an educational system that is basically engaged in turning out nonworld citizens. What might be called the "our gang" approach to the human experience permeates our schools and those of other countries as well. It is strongly reenforced by indoctrination at home and conditioning throughout society.

The education of the small child, both at home and in school, naturally starts with the near and the familiar. It emphasizes the family and the community. It goes on to build up a sense of emotional attachment to and identification with the city, the state, and the nation. This is all perfectly natural and commendable. These are necessary groupings. The nation has become the most important unit of organization in modern times, and I believe strong patterns of identification with and loyalty to the nation will be necessary for the effective operation of all societies, at least for the immediately foreseeable future.

The problem is that, at this time, when the world community is rapidly superseding the nation as the ultimate unit of human cooperation, we do so little to build

* From A Child's Garden of Verses, by Robert Louis Stevenson, Oxford University Press, 1966 edition.

a sense of identification with the whole human race and emotional attachment to a world community. Such attitudes will be necessary if the global unit is to serve as one of survival rather than destruction. Consider the discrepancy between the overwhelming mass of influences that give a national orientation to the young and the feeble efforts to produce an international, intercultural orientation. The symbols of the one—the national flag, the national anthem, the pledge of allegiance, and many more—are constantly present; the symbols of the other are virtually nonexistent. Hyperbole and boasting about the nation are the common coin of speech for politicians and many others; suspicion and skepticism are the accepted approaches to the outside world. Formal schooling centers on the American way of life, blatantly proclaimed or at least tacitly assumed to be superior to all others. Repeatedly, the school child is led through the story of American history, often as a tale of ever-victorious conflict between our country and other national groupings. The rest of the human race gets short historical shrift, except as the setting for our national story or as the background for our national achievements as the ultimate flowering of Western civilization. What chance does a sixth-grade program in some selected foreign countries and cultures have, not to counteract the national orientation of education, but to add to it an equally necessary international orientation? Such programs are clearly too little and too late.

Some may argue that the young themselves are correcting this situation. A sort of reaction has appeared among many college and high-school students against the overwhelming emphasis on our nation and the touting of its superiority. It has become common among young people in the United States, and in some other industrialized societies as well, to criticize their own nation and look beyond it for trans-national ideals and loyalties. All this may show that youth senses a need for something more than the old national unit of organization.

The whole movement, however, seems to me to be much clearer in its negative condemnations than in its positive affirmations. It seems less a realization of the need for an international community and a truly felt sense of world citizenship than a reaction against the specific society in which the young person finds himself. In part, the reaction seems to be against the frustrating complexities of modern life and the puzzling multiplicity of choices for a generation raised in relative affluence at a time of seemingly unlimited technological possibilities. In part, the reaction may be against the naïve oversell, whether it be of national glory or wonder drugs, from a generation made sophisticated and skeptical by television advertising. While many young Americans are quick to point out the "hypocrisy" of American society—meaning the gap between ideals and realities—the international ideals and loyalties they espouse in place of national ones seem to me superficial. They are rarely based on much knowledge and appear to be expressions more of inward-directed frustration than of real fellow feeling for others.

The person, young or old, who flaunts his rejection of his own country by adopting what is regarded there as an outlandish costume or life style does not necessarily win insights thereby into other nations or cultures, which are likely to regard his adoption of their supposed attitudes and style of dress as even more outlandish. The actions of such persons may be therapeutic for themselves, but they do not build bridges between cultures. For the problems we are considering in this book, they are stepping stones to nowhere.

Hatred for what one knows intimately is a poor basis for love of what is less known. Nor is the rejection of national identity and loyalty the real road to the building of a broader sense of identity and loyalty. Identification with the nation state was not produced by wiping out family bonds and local pride. It was added to these. Similarly, identification with the world community cannot simply be substituted for identification with the nation. As far as one can peer into the future, both will be necessary for human survival.

The overly parochial approach in education in and out of school is by no means limited to a narrow nationalistic emphasis. Its more insidious forms stress racial, cultural, and even religious groupings. Where international communities are starting to form, they tend to be within a common racial, cultural, and religious type. This is true of the European Community, the most successful development along these lines. As I have pointed out, the strains in the triangular community are greatest between its one non-Western, non-Christian, non-Caucasian member and the rest. Religion, culture, and race throughout history have been seen as sharply dividing peoples from one another. When these divisions exist within a single country, they often produce conflicts and instability. Between nations, they commonly strengthen lines of national cleavage. Thus, in the effort to build a world community, cultural, religious, and racial feelings of exclusiveness may in the long run prove more difficult to overcome than national prejudices.

What I have called the parochial approach to education in the United States actually combines an emphasis on the nation with emphases on these broader but also exclusive in-groups. Back of the national unit, "right or wrong" but always triumphant, is the much wider religious unit of Christendom (together with its mother religion Judaism, but not its brother religion Islam), and almost synonymous with the religious unit are the cultural one of Western civilization and the closely parallel unit of the white race, which, though perhaps little mentioned, lurks in the background.

Most people are probably not conscious that our traditional education is overwhelmingly about our own particular group, and thus tends to build a strong sense of identity with it, to the exclusion of the other members of the human race who do not qualify for membership. But stop and think a moment. Except for the recent attempts to include in the curriculum something about other nations and cultures, how much has there been about nations and cultures not part of our direct heritage? How many great figures of history outside this one cultural legacy can the average schoolboy name? How do the other nations and cultures figure except as barbarian threats, peripheral influences, or subject territories of the one true civilization?

Egyptians and Babylonians, who obviously were part of our own cultural heritage, figure almost as much as oppressors of the Old Testament Hebrews, whose cultural ancestry we feel more strongly. Persians and Carthaginians, who were close to our cultural line, appear primarily as threats to the true "homes of civilization" in Greece and Rome. The Huns, as Asiatics, were obviously worse than good, clean Nordic "barbarians" and thus were even more responsible for bringing on the "dark ages." Then come the Arab infidels, the Mongol hordes, and the "unspeakable" Turks who menaced Christendom, the American Indians who by the laws of God and nature had to be replaced by civilized white men, and the teeming millions of the Orient who provided the West with markets and empires and now trouble it with problems of undernourishment and instability. But where in our education are the Isaiahs and Platos of the other parts of the world, their Alexanders and Napoleons, their Dantes and Shakespeares, their Giottos and Rembrandts, their triumphs of political organization, their cultural Renaissances, their great insights in religion, ethics, and social organization?

The lack is not noticed by most people. Even the more sophisticated may have such a deep, if politely unexpressed, conviction of the superiority of their own cultural grouping to all others that, while they may be ready to accept a little tokenism about other peoples and their cultures, they know in their heart of hearts that everything really worthwhile in civilization is to be found in its highest form in the West. Let me give just one specific illustration. Not long ago there was a magnificent television series about the Western Christian artistic tradition. I personally enjoyed it very much. But it had for me one deep annoyance. Its title was simply *Civilization*, as if the Western Christian tradition were the whole of human civilization. Repeatedly it made mention of those outside this tradition as barbarians threatening to snuff out "civilization." These are mere peccadilloes in a superb television series, and the author in the Foreword to the book that followed the television series did apologize for the use of the title *Civilization*, when no consideration had been given to anything outside the Western Christian tradition. But the fact that this title seemed at all acceptable for the historical presentation of only a single cultural tradition shows how sublimely ethnocentric even our sophisticates can be. No wonder the schoolboy accepts without question the "our gang" approach to the human experience.

The question remains how best to correct the situation. I enter into this subject with some diffidence, since my knowledge of the techniques and problems of elementary and secondary education is thin. But let me offer some general suggestions. I do not think the situation can be corrected simply by additions to the curriculum. In this age of rapidly expanding frontiers of knowledge and growing complexities in life, school curriculums are already overburdened. It would be impossible to give normal students in the usual period of education a soundly balanced view of the world community and a sense of world citizenship by adding to a core curriculum about one nation and its cultural background adequate consideration of other nations and cultures. Additions would of necessity have to be very selective, leaving large lacunae in coverage; and, being additions to the central core of study, they would tend to underline difference rather than identities. The net result might be simply to impress the child with the idea that others do things differently, which in his perceptions, as encouraged by his home and local environment, is likely to mean the wrong way.

A more basic reform in education will be necessary.

This I believe should be a conscious effort to get away from the assumed, even if unspecified, unit of our own nation and its culture as the almost exclusive focus of education. To put it in more positive terms, we should broaden the focus to include all humanity and the whole of the human experience. Basically what is needed is a profound change in the underlying assumptions of the curriculum planners, the textbook writers, and teachers. Change in the specific content of education would automatically follow, and students would find no difficulty in adjusting in turn. If they can understand the great abstraction of the nation, they can certainly understand humanity too, for it is a much less arbitrary unit.

Actually, the content of education might not change greatly, though it would be sorted out somewhat differently. While man as a whole would be the object of study, the child's own nation and culture, with which he must become familiar, would naturally be used as the chief source on the human experience. But these materials would not be presented in terms of a unique story of a presumably "chosen" people, who always demonstrated their spiritual superiority, if not necessarily their military dominance, over the "unchosen" multitudes. They would be presented as one example of the many ways in which men have responded to new problems and new opportunities as their technological skills increased, their social organization became more complex, and their concepts more diverse and sophisticated. Some of the other responses at other times and in other societies would also have to be presented on a selective basis to make the problems and choices meaningful. But this would not add greatly to the total content. The important point is that these responses of others would be included in the central core of education as equally valid parts of the human experience, not as peripheral variants to the authentic main line of "civilization" that we ourselves are assumed to represent.

I am suggesting a basically comparative rather than unilinear approach to the human experience. Through it, the child would learn what he needs to know about his own country and culture, but he would perceive them as part of a broader human experience. They would be seen as one of the many responses of men to the needs and problems of family relations, economic production, and political organization; to communication through language and writing; to esthetic expression in literature, art, music, and dance; to the gropings to understand the meaning and values of life; and to the need to solve conflicts and rationalize the relations among ever larger and more complex social and political units.

Such a comparative approach to the human experience would produce a less sharply defined story of our own national and cultural unit and might lose a good bit of the romance of history. There would be less of George Washington cutting down a cherry tree and throwing a dollar across the Delaware River, or of Henry VIII shucking off his various wives. But it might in compensation pick up some other stories of equal interest. The eighth-century emperor Hsüan Tsung, his beautiful consort Yang-kuei-fei, and her favorite, the "barbarian" general An Lu-shan, make a historical triangle as fascinating as Plantagenet or Tudor intrigues. In any case, students today learn very little of the sweep of the traditional, nationally oriented, culture-bound history, and much of what is taught along these lines is, after all, myth rather than reality.

A more serious objection would be that a comparative approach might lessen interest and pride somewhat in the specific achievements of one's own nation and culture. My basic point, however, is that this sort of narrow pride has to be diminished a little. The traditional, unilinear approach to the human experience stands in the way of an understanding of the broad diversity of human experience, a realization of the great complexity of human problems, an appreciation of what man as a whole has achieved, and the development of a sense of common human identity and world citizenship. Such attitudes will probably be far more useful in the early twenty-first century than narrow pride and interest in one's own specific national and cultural tradition and its story of conflict with other groups. If that sort of narrow and uninformed parochial pride continues too strongly into the twenty-first century, it will undoubtedly be a hazard to mankind's survival.

The change in attitudes that is needed does not differ greatly from similar shifts man has made in the past, except for the speed with which it must be accomplished. Not so long ago, men comprehended the human historical experience solely in terms of individual personalities and clashing royal lines. Only in recent times was it discovered that beneath these superficial surface phenomena were larger economic, social, and intellectual currents moving whole nations. The human experience then came to be interpreted, not so much as the story of a few heroic or divinely ordained individuals, but as the massive evolution of peoples and nations. I am suggesting that we now need to move on to a new stage and see it not as the story of conflicting nations but of humanity as a whole. We might gain a more meaningful concept of the human historical experience if, instead of concentrating exclusively on one cultural and national current, we analyzed the various facets of human problems and achievements at the different levels of technical skills, guiding concepts, and social organization that man has passed through. The difficulties and potentialities differ widely between a neolithic society, a preindustrial subsistence-agricultural country, and a modern industrialized urbanized nation. Contemporary American problems and possibilities can be better understood through comparisons with those of Germany, Japan, or the Soviet Union than by comparisons with Rome, Tudor England, or even the early American Republic.

I might cite two other advantages of the comparative approach to the human experience over the unilinear. One is that it would help to reveal the interrelations between the various aspects of a specific social system or cultural pattern—that is, the fact that a change in one factor is very likely to have an impact on others. The second is that it would help illustrate the continuous nature of human problems—that the solution of one problem usually produces new ones and the crossing of one mountain range of opportunity brings others into sight. In this age of accelerating change, when the rising generation faces an unpredictable future, the understanding of these two points may be of far greater value than is much of the factual baggage we have been carrying in our traditional system of education.

Let me try to give some illustrations of a comparative approach to the human experience. Insofar as we include in education anything about the primitive stages of civilization, we already make it comparative. No one appears to be personally possessive about his own ancestral cavemen. The transitions from paleolithic hunter to neolithic farmer, to the Bronze Age and the Early Iron Age, are usually described as being advances made by mankind. But thereafter the focus usually narrows to one specific cultural or even national tradition to the exclusion of the rest.

This narrowing of the subject matter leads to an unnecessary cultural impoverishment. The child's appreciation of literature, art, music, and dance might be greatly increased by widening the focus to all mankind and not limiting it to one cultural tradition. The effort to award as many of the cultural gold medals as possible to one's own national or cultural unit is a childish absurdity we should get beyond. Beethoven enriches the lives of Japanese and Africans as well as Germans. The Pyramids, Greek sculpture, the Olmec art of Ancient Mexico, the Buddhist and Hindu rock sculptures and architecture of India, the Sung landscapes of China, the cathedral of Chartres, the medieval gardens of Japan, Renaissance painting, Persian miniatures, and African wood carving are all part of a common human heritage and should figure in education accordingly. Who can tell which of these will strike the strongest esthetic chords in the twenty-first century?

All human achievements should be regarded as the common legacy of all men. The modern scientific method is no less essential to Koreans and Pakistanis than to Europeans or Americans; Indian philosophic subtleties and African musical rhythms can be as enriching to other peoples as to those who first developed them. Paper and printing are no less valuable to Westerners for having been invented by Chinese. Why do we ignore their story and leave with the child the impression that printing began with Gutenberg, when Chinese had been printing books for seven centuries before his time? We all share in these human achievements and should take equal pride in them.

In the field of human relations, one wonders if the young student can grasp the meaning of the family in society only from what he sees of the family in his particular corner of the United States or what he may learn of the decay of family solidarity in recent American history. Would he not acquire a better concept of this very basic unit of human organization by learning about a more varied sampling of family patterns—the traditional and contemporary Chinese family, the family in feudal society, the family in industrial Germany and Japan, the family in tribal African society?

Or take basic political organization. When presented as a description of what we ourselves have right now, it may be both dull and unrevealing of the real problems, because to the child it seems obvious and inevitable. But analyze it in comparative terms and it becomes more interesting as the real questions begin to appear. Our concept of law derives heavily from Rome and also from medieval feudal notions, but a comparison with other legal traditions and judicial systems would be instructive.

Modern governments depend on great bureaucracies, and here the key experience is that of the Chinese, who since ancient times have attempted to select through state examinations a bureaucracy of educated, morally upright men. This basic concept has been applied to modern civil service systems in far more perfected form than the United States can boast in such countries as Germany, France, and Japan. To have much understanding of representative government through elections, which is such a fundamental element in our modern political system, the student would have to know something about the very profound differences both in elections and in leadership between parliamentary and presidential democracies, between proportional representation systems and winner-take-all systems like ours, and between electorates that are highly educated and well served by the mass media and those that are not, as in the case of India.

Even in the search for value and meaning in life, something beyond our own cultural tradition should be included in education. We will probably look most to the Hebrew prophets, the Greek philosophers, Christianity, and the later Western thinkers. But our understanding of the problems involved could be made much deeper through some consideration of the other great efforts along this line—the Hindu, Buddhist, Confucian, and Taoist perceptions that paralleled in time those of the Hebrew prophets and the Greek philosophers, the Islamic version of the basic Western concept of God and man's relation to Him, and the later philosophical ideas of the various non-Western traditions.

It must be admitted, of course, that recently many young and adult Americans have shown a tremendous interest in the Indian *yoga* tradition, the ancient Chinese classic of the *I-ching*, the Japanese form of Zen Buddhism, and a number of other philosophic and religious currents from non-Western cultures. This phenomenon suggests that there is a real need or at least a great openness among Americans to learn more about the values and spiritual insights of other peoples. Conversely, the philosophical, political, social, and economic concepts of the West have become a common intellectual coin in sophisticated circles throughout the world. In these two ways there is a great deal more of the intellectual and spiritual interaction that a world community must have than there was only a few decades ago. But most of this interchange has developed outside the formal educational systems, except for its highest levels. If these needs and possibilities exist at the higher levels, they also should be appropriately reflected throughout the lower levels of education.

The paragraphs above are in no sense an outline of how elementary and secondary education should be reshaped but simply a few scattered illustrations. Only specialists in the field can undertake the task of restructuring education in order to develop a sense of world citizenship in young people and prepare them better for life in the twenty-first century. There will have to be a great deal of careful analysis of the problems and considerable experimentation. Close cooperation between curriculum designers, textbook writers, and teachers will of course be needed, but cooperation between these groups and experts in the study of other cultures will be even more necessary. As I have pointed out, the gap between the forward edge of scholarship and elementary and secondary education represents a serious time lag in our fast-moving age. In the major shift of approach I am advocating, a comparable gap might wreck the whole effort.

There is one other basic educational reform I would put forward as having relevance for the development of a sense of world citizenship. This is an increase in language study. I have already mentioned the command of foreign languages as necessary for expert knowledge and also as valuable for the average informed citizen in gaining some understanding of the outside world. It may be even more important as a key element for producing a sense of world citizenship.

No experience is more culturally broadening than the learning of a foreign language. Nothing proves more convincingly that there are people in the world who do things differently from us. The child can be told in English about how Chinese differ from us and still not really absorb the lesson; but if he studies the Chinese language and writing system, the lesson will undoubtedly sink in. And it will not be just that Chinese are different from us, speaking English, for example, with a funny accent. It will be that we are different from Chinese and find it hard to speak and write a language they handle with ease.

The study of a foreign language can be very chastening to arrogant parochialism. The arbitrary absolutes of pronunciation, vocabulary, and grammar of another language reveal how arbitrary is our own language, which seems to us ordained by the laws of God and nature and the rules of logic. The well-turned phrase of one language, when put into another, turns out to be only an untranslatable and sometimes silly pun. The logical necessity of the one becomes the illogical grammatical rule of another. A foreign language may be the first steps of the ladder out of the cultural well in which most human frogs live.

I doubt that the average monolingual person will ever be able to appreciate the diversity of humanity and the need for mutual adjustments. He will not be prepared to be a world citizen but, in the pattern of the nineteenth century, is likely to expect others to join his own narrow world. Thus the reintroduction of foreign language study on a large scale into our educational system may be as important in building a sense of world citizenship as the restructuring of the content of education I have discussed above.

Foreign language instruction should come early in the educational process, basically at the elementary level. This is because it can serve as a fundamental shaper of the child's perception of the world. It can help him accept the fact that there is much in the world that differs greatly from what he sees around him and to which he must learn to accommodate himself. It should come early also because the young child learns a foreign language with ease and pleasure. At that stage it can be one of the really fun elements in education, not the meaningless drudgery it has seemed to generations of students who took it up later in their schooling.

The modern, more efficient techniques of language teaching through native speakers and electronic audiovisual aids also are particularly effective with young children. At that age it is natural for them to learn a foreign language through imitation and repetition, as they did with their native language. The older they become, the more resistant they are to this process and the more dependent on a rational effort to substitute the foreign language, element by element, for the patterns of language already established in their minds, becoming in the process grammarians more than speakers.

The question of which languages should be studied is probably less important than when they should be studied. One criterion in the selection of a foreign language would be foreseeable utility in later life. From this point of view, Spanish, French, German, and Italian would seem natural favorites for Americans. Another criterion would be differentness from English. The greater the difference, the more value will be derived from the experience, both in terms of understanding the diversity of the world and in realizing the logical limitations of any language. An overlapping of the practical utility and difference factors would point toward such important but very different languages as Japanese, Chinese, Arabic, Hindi, Swahili, and Russian.

Foreign language study, I realize, is at present an unpopular cause. It is regarded as unstimulating rote memory work of little relevance for most young people. These criticisms do have considerable validity when leveled at the conception and practice of much foreign language instruction in our schools today. But if properly understood and implemented, the teaching of foreign languages could be a key element in preparing the next generation for successful membership in the emerging world community.

My remarks about the need for foreign language study as well as the more basic point about a broader cultural focus in education are not meant to be prescriptive but merely illustrative. The next generation clearly will need more knowledge and understanding about the rest of the world and a greater sense of world community than the present generation of leaders possesses. For this, some basic reforms in education will be necessary. I have merely suggested some points that seem to me important, but these require much greater development, and there may be many other points of equal validity. We need careful thought and a great deal of effort if education is to rise to the challenge.

My greatest fear is that, engrossed as we are in a multitude of seemingly more pressing problems, we will fail to act on these problems which seem less immediately threatening because of their longer time fuse. In the global situation there is right now no clearly identifiable enemy staring us down a gun barrel. Instead, there are only some rather dimly perceived Frankenstein monsters, such as global pollution, an imbalance between population and natural resources, and the widening gap between the industrialized affluent nations and the less developed countries, lurking down our path a generation or two ahead.

We are strongly conditioned by the conventional wisdom that problems should be met as they arise. This did suffice for a slower moving era, but it will not do for ours. In this age of vast and extraordinarily complex global interrelationships, by the time the truly difficult international problems have fully surfaced, they are all too likely to be beyond solution. We obviously must handle our immediate problems, but we also must prepare for those that lie ahead. Adequate international understanding and a sense of world citizenship will require a lead time of a full generation or more—some years to restructure education and then two decades for its products to mature into responsible and influential citizens.

In any case, there may be less of a contrast than is assumed between the immediately pressing domestic social and educational problems within the United States and the longer range international problem of developing greater understanding and a realization of the needs of the emerging world community. The effort to make education focus on mankind as a whole and to develop a sense of world citizenship may appear to lead in the opposite direction from the current emphasis in the United States on the local community and distinctive ethnic roots. The one seems to stress universalism, the other particularism. But are these really conflicting trends? If we perceive ourselves less as members of exclusive, competing national and ethnic groups and more as the diverse heirs of human civilization as a whole, may we not simultaneously help to lessen the tensions between the divergent minorities and the dominant majority within our country?

A sense of world citizenship embracing all national groupings and the acceptance of ethnic diversity within our own nation are really two sides of the same coin. Both accent the universality of man and help place the national unit in proper perspective as only one of several successive levels of human organization. The focus on mankind and his civilization as the subject of education includes the ethnic minorities in a way that a narrow focus on the dominant national tradition does not. They, too, share fully in this common human heritage. A realization of this point could make their search for identity less agonizing to them and less threatening to others. Thus education for world citizenship could prove of great value in this seemingly very different direction.

I do not rest my case, however, on this important by-product of the educational reforms I have been discussing. Wholly aside from the domestic American situation, a reorientation of education so as to give young people everywhere a sense of the shared interests and basic oneness of mankind and to prepare them for effective participation as members of a world community is, I believe, a clear necessity for human survival in the twenty-first century. The United States with its great ethnic diversity and its huge international involvements has a special opportunity to play a major role in this great educational breakthrough.

A Note About the Author

Edwin O. Reischauer, since September 1966 a University Professor at Harvard University, served with distinction as United States Ambassador to Japan from 1961 to 1966. His mission was the culmination of long experience in East Asia. He was born in Tokyo in 1910, lived in Japan until 1927, and has returned many times since then for study and visits to Japan, as well as to China, Korea, and other areas in the Far East. He received his A.B. degree from Oberlin College in 1931 and his Ph.D. from Harvard in 1939. In the interval, he studied at the universities of Paris, Tokyo, and Kyoto, and in Korea and China. He became an instructor at Harvard in 1939, an associate professor in 1945, and professor of Japanese history in 1950. During World War II, he served with the rank of lieutenant colonel in the Military Intelligence Service of the War Department General Staff. Professor Reischauer has also worked for the Department of State in the Division of Far Eastern Affairs. He was director of the Harvard-Yenching Institute from 1956 to 1961 and has been the Chairman of its Board of Trustees since 1969. He served as president of the Association for Asian Studies from 1955 to 1956. Among his books are *Japan Past and Present* (1947, new and revised editions 1952, 1964), revised under a new title, *Japan: The Story of a Nation* (1970); *Beyond Vietnam: The United States and Asia* (1967); *The United States and Japan* (1950, 1957, 1965); *Wanted: An Asian Policy* (1955); *Ennin's Travels in T'ang China* (1955); with J. K. Fairbank, *East Asia: The Great Tradition* (1960); and with J. K. Fairbank and A. M. Craig, *East Asia: The Modern Transformation* (1965) and *East Asia: Tradition and Transformation* (1973).

VINTAGE POLITICAL SCIENCE
AND SOCIAL CRITICISM

VINTAGE WORKS OF SCIENCE
AND PSYCHOLOGY

VINTAGE CRITICISM,
LITERATURE, MUSIC, AND ART

VINTAGE BELLES—LETTRES

VINTAGE BIOGRAPHY AND AUTOBIOGRAPHY